About the Author

Jonathan Milman has been working in the education space for the past decade, ensuring that thousands of students achieve their dreams and obtain entrance to their chosen vocation and chosen college. This book is a culmination of his knowledge that he has accumulated over the years.

Jonathan Milman

Gail Rayham

Acknowledgements

I would like to thank all of the members who had a hand in making this book happen over the years. Anton Cernokulski, aside from writing a ton of problems and chapters, you convinced me that writing this book using LaTeX would produce not only the best results, but allow me to enjoy the process. Lolita Rozenbaum for managing the creation and ensuring that my vision for creating a unique guide to the SAT's would be realized.

A special thank you goes to Adelina Zaripova, who not only was instrumental in ensuring this book was fully edited and the answer key matched the problems, but helped update this book to the new format of the Digital SAT.

Table of Contents

10 Things you NEED to Know for the Grammar Portion of the SAT 1

Scoring 2

Conversion Table 2

The Book 3

Most Common Topics 4

List of Rhetorical and Grammatical Questions 4

Transition Words 5

Sentence Structure 9

Commas! 12

Modifiers 13

Commonly used words after commas 18

Lists 22

Appositives 28

Comma Nouns/Pronouns 32

SEMI-COLONS 37

,CONJUNCTIONS 41

COLONS 45

HYPHENS 49

PARENTHESES 53

ACTIVE VS. PASSIVE VOICE 56

Who/Whom 57

Affect vs. Effect 61

CONCISION 65

PRONOUNS 68

Replace a Pronoun with the Noun 69

I vs. Me 72

Tenses 76

Past-Present-Future 76

Verb-Tense Consistency 79

False Comparison 82

Apostrophe 86

Commonly Misused Words 90

Quotes 93

Answer Key 97

10 Things you NEED to Know for the Grammar Portion of the SAT

Cheat: Things you NEED to know!

1. In the New Digital SAT, grammar questions have been integrated into the Reading and Writing Portion of the SAT.
2. This does not mean that grammar is an unessential topic to study.
3. In terms of the Reading and Writing Portion, you have 64 minutes to complete both modules - 32 minutes for each module
4. Each module of the Reading and Writing Portion consists of 27 Questions - 54 Questions total. You will see approximately 15 Reading questions and 12 Grammar Questions per module.
5. The exam is adaptive, which means that if you do well on the first Module, the second module will be harder.
6. Harder questions are worth more, therefore the harder the exam, the higher you can score.
7. Not everything written in the passages is important.
8. The answer is not always found in the text and some of the problems will require you to use outside information or infer.
9. Every word within the answer choices is crucial
10. Be as literal as possible!
11. Never Disagree or Agree with the text, just read it for what it is and answer the question.
12. Never Leave a Question Blank! Always try to answer every single question on the SAT. Ideally, you will be able to narrow each question down to at least two choices. However, always make sure every question at least is filled in!
13. You should never have extra time left over.
14. Time is never a problem if you know what you're doing!

Scoring

Let's just say you take an physics exam and the teacher makes the exam too difficult. When I mean too difficult, imagine that the highest grade in the class is a 50% out of 100%. Will the professor fail everyone? Of course he can't because it will make him look bad. So, what is he to do... Curve!
An exam curve is a way to level out the scores based on standard deviation and other mathematical factors that relate to average and median that won't be explained throughout this book. All that you need to know is that the worse the people do on the exam, the higher the curve.

The SAT is graded on a curve!

Curves vary depending on how well the student body does on that particular exam and can vary greatly from exam to exam. Unfortunately, there is no way to predict how well one curve is to another and if anyone says that the exam has a better curve from month to month, they are simply lying to you or do not know what they are talking about.

However, we can generalize and effectively say that the harder questions are worth more, simply because of the fact that there are less students that will get them right. Thus, the exam is graded accordingly. Below is what a sample conversion table looks like, where the raw score is simply the number of correct answers and you must look to the right to understand the math or reading scale.

Conversion Table

Raw Score Conversion Table: Section Scores

RAW SCORE	Reading and Writing Section Score Range		Math Section Score Range	
(# OF CORRECT ANSWERS)	LOWER	UPPER	LOWER	UPPER
0	200	200	200	200
1	200	200	200	200
2	200	200	200	200
3	200	200	200	200
4	200	200	200	200
5	200	200	200	200
6	200	200	200	200
7	200	210	200	220
8	200	220	200	230
9	210	230	220	250
10	230	250	250	280
11	240	260	280	310
12	250	270	290	320
13	260	280	300	330
14	280	300	310	340
15	290	310	320	350
16	320	340	330	360
17	340	360	330	360
18	350	370	340	370
19	360	380	350	380
20	370	390	360	390
21	370	390	370	400
22	380	400	370	400
23	390	410	380	410
24	400	420	390	420
25	410	430	400	430
26	420	440	420	450
27	420	440	430	460
28	430	450	440	470
29	440	460	460	490
30	450	470	470	500
31	460	480	480	510
32	460	480	500	530
33	470	490	510	540
34	480	500	520	550
35	490	510	530	560
36	490	510	550	580
37	500	520	560	590
38	510	530	570	600
39	520	540	580	610
40	530	550	590	620
41	540	560	600	630
42	540	560	620	650
43	550	570	630	660
44	560	580	650	680
45	570	590	670	700
46	580	600	690	720
47	590	610	710	740
48	590	610	730	760
49	600	620	740	770
50	610	630	750	780
51	620	640	760	790
52	630	650	770	800
53	630	650	780	800
54	640	660	790	800
55	650	670		
56	660	680		
57	670	690		
58	680	700		
59	690	710		
60	700	720		
61	710	730		
62	720	740		
63	730	750		
64	750	770		
65	770	790		
66	790	800		

The Book

This Book is very unique in a few ways:

1. It is first designed to fit the needs of the individual student who wants to learn applicable grammar question-answering strategies for the Reading and Writing portion of the Digital SAT.

2. This is not just going to be a bunch of practice exams! Instead, the book will guide you just as though you were sitting inside a live SAT class and help you through every passage.

3. Every question and passage will be explained based on strategic concepts that are taught throughout the book. Never will you simply be explained that you should refer to a portion of the passage. Instead, you will be taught how you should be thinking on this portion of the exam to maximize your results.

Now, let's discuss some of the key features of this book:

1. **This is a Workbook!** If you have obtained the online edition, please make sure to print it. Otherwise, you can use a writing program to write while you are reading. DO NOT passively work through this book as it will hinder your learning process. Take notes and practice diligently!

2. **Definitions, Rules, and Cheats:** All of the most important concepts are outlined for you to be the most convenient for review.

Definitions
These are things that you just need to understand and remember.

Rules
Concepts that need to be followed and the essential rules governing each topic.

Cheats
Key strategies that you can follow to answer questions in the most effective and efficient manner possible.

Now, it's time to begin...

Most Common Topics: Grammar

Review each rule and learn to apply and see what type of questions you may potentially get on those topics. There are two major categories of questions you need to master on the Grammar portion:

Definition: Rhetorical Questions

Questions that will ask you whether or not you understand the author's tone, meaning, and overall argument.
These questions always involve some text prior to the questions.

Definition: Grammatical Questions

These questions only focus on grammar rules and can only be mastered by mastering the rules.
These questions require you to read no text and to simply input some sort of punctuation.

List of Rhetorical and Grammatical Questions

Rhetorical Questions

1. Transition Word Problems
2. Vocabulary and Style & Tone
3. Logic Problems

Grammatical Questions

1. Sentence Structure
2. Comma Issues
   (a) , Noun/Pronoun
   (b) Modifiers
   (c) Lists
   (d) Appositive
   (e) Commonly used words after commas
3. Semi-Colons
4. , Conjunctions
5. Colons
6. Hyphens
7. Parentheses
8. Active vs. Passive
   (a) Who/Whom, They/Them, He/Him/She/Her
   (b) Affect vs. Effect
9. Concision
10. Pronouns
11. Tense
    (a) Past-Present-Future
    (b) Verb Tense Consistency
12. False Comparison
13. Apostrophe
14. Commonly Misused Words
15. Quotes

Transition Words

These questions always involve a word, phrase, or conjunction that starts a sentence, followed by a comma.
Read the previous sentence and check to make sure that the word, phrase, or conjunction transitions the ideas into the next sentence well. Luckily, there are only three ways the SAT likes to use transition words:

Continuation - **Causing** - **Contrasting**

Cheat: Transition Words

Addition	Contrast	Causation
Also	However	Thus
Moreover	On the other hand	As such
In fact	Nonetheless	Therefore
Furthermore	Nevertheless	Consequently
In Addition	Still	As a result
Similarly	Instead	
Indeed	Despite this	
In Conclusion	Meanwhile	
In other words		
Finally		
Next		
Likewise		
Then		
For example		

Let's work through some sample problems.

Sample Problems

Justice Stephen Johnson Field widened the interpretation of "papers" in the Fourth Amendment to incorporate sealed letters conveyed through the postal service, and ________ established a constitutional concept for postal regulations. This ruling then became the foundation for Justice Brandeis's comparison of private phone calls to sealed letters.

1. Which choice completes the text with the most logical transition?

   (a) moreover

   (b) thus

   (c) conversely,

   (d) meanwhile,

In certain situations, such as job interviews and client meetings, it is expected that one will dress in a professional manner. ________ some professions, like law enforcement, necessitate uniforms that are free of individualized modifications.

2. Which choice completes the text with the most logical transition?

   (a) On the other hand,

   (b) Furthermore,

   (c) Incidentally,

   (d) Conversely,

Practice Problems: Transition Words

Scholars of the increasing field of behavioral economics have various theories, namely that humans are not logical when it comes to finances. In reality, individuals make illogical economic decisions regularly. ________ investigating the behavior of saving has revealed that a substantial amount of employees decide not to join retirement-savings plans even when it is beneficial to them.

1. Which choice completes the text with the most logical transition?

   (a) However

   (b) Moreover,

   (c) In other words,

   (d) For instance,

An electronic health record system can help reduce medical mistakes by cross-referencing drug details and offering automated alerts about potential adverse drug interactions. ________ at Brigham and Women's Hospital in Boston, MA, the occurrence of major medical errors was reduced by over half once the electronic system was set up.

2. Which choice completes the text with the most logical transition?

   (a) Likewise

   (b) Still,

   (c) In this case,

   (d) In fact,

Levine and Rocco took steps to make sure that the job-sharing arrangement they were providing would give continuity and constancy to employees under their management. "It is essential for us to be consistent," they stated. ________ they agreed to work for three days every week, with Wednesday as the day of overlap.

3. Which choice completes the text with the most logical transition?

   (a) Nevertheless,

   (b) To this end,

   (c) However,

   (d) Similarly,

On June 20, 1965, a buzz of anticipation echoed through an auditorium in Kingston, Jamaica, as a sizable gathering had come together for the University of the West Indies commencement services. In addition to the 400 graduates, many people had come to listen to the words of the day's commencement speaker, the Reverend Dr. Martin Luther King Jr. __________ the audience members, who were familiar with Dr.Kings widespread campaign to increase civil rights in America, were thrilled to see Dr.King rise to the podium a mere few feet away from them.

4. Which choice completes the text with the most logical transition?
   (a) Furthermore
   (b) As a result,
   (c) By contrast,
   (d) Unfortunately

The Cat in the Hat first came to life when William Spaulding felt the need for more captivating books for youthful readers. He then arranged to have dinner with Theodor Giesel, who wrote and illustrated kids books under the name "Dr. Suess", and gave him the difficult task of writing a book that first graders wouldn't be able to put down! Giesel had already published many childrens books and had even received three nominations for the highly esteemed Caldecott Medal, so he certainly had plenty of experience. __________ this new project provided him with a complication - Spaulding asked him to compose the book solely using a restricted primary school vocabulary.

5. Which choice completes the text with the most logical transition?
   (a) However,
   (b) For example,
   (c) Furthermore,
   (d) At any rate,

After the American Civil War, a vast number of African American ex-slaves left the American South and moved to the West in search of better lives. This mass movement was known as the Great Exodus. A majority of these individuals established farming villages, but faced a lot of hardships. During the initial years, their harvests were not enough to sustain their livelihoods; therefore, they had to ask for assistance from the people in the area or the state government. The success of the exoduster settlements was directly tied to the yield of their farms. __________ their harvests increased, allowing them to buy food, lumber, and other items.

6. Which choice completes the text with the most logical transition?
   (a) In time,
   (b) Still,
   (c) Rather,
   (d) Next,

During the 19th century, two eminent English Romanticist landscapists, John Constable and J.M.W. Turner, had a competitive relationship. This tension became more acute in 1831, and then further escalated when their works were exhibited next to each other at the 1832 Royal Academy Exhibition. Constable's *The Opening of Waterloo Bridge"* was a colorful and precise painting; Turner's *Helvoetsulys*, __________ was a much more subdued piece with predominantly white and grey shades.

7. Which choice completes the text with the most logical transition?

   (a) ultimately,

   (b) furthermore,

   (c) by contrast,

   (d) in fact,

The Sun emits blue light during the day, and this wavelength is similar to what is given off by technological gadgets like computers, TVs, and phones. The blue light causes the eye to send a chemical message to the suprachiasmatic nucleus (SCN) which leads to increases in alertness, temperature, and pulse. __________these reactions in our bodies are the same as what happens when we are exposed to daylight.

8. Which choice completes the text with the most logical transition?

   (a) Nevertheless,

   (b) However,

   (c) Therefore,

   (d) Further,

The Theory of Evolution, proposed by Charles Darwin, revolutionized the biological sciences. Darwin introduced the concept of natural selection, explaining how species adapt and evolve over time. His ideas challenged the prevailing views of his era, sparking debates and discussions across scientific and religious communities. __________ Darwin's work laid the foundation for modern evolutionary biology and influenced numerous scientific fields.

9. Which choice completes the text with the most logical transition?

   (a) Nevertheless,

   (b) Consequently,

   (c) Additionally,

   (d) On the contrary,

The development of the internet has transformed global communication and information exchange. Initially conceived as a project to connect military and academic computers, it has grown into a vast network linking billions of devices worldwide. The advent of social media platforms further expanded its impact, enabling instant sharing of information and ideas across the globe. __________ this digital revolution has raised concerns about privacy, data security, and the digital divide.

10. Which choice completes the text with the most logical transition?

    (a) However,

    (b) For instance,

    (c) Similarly,

    (d) Therefore,

Sample Problems: Solutions and Explanations

1. **Correct Answer: B** In this example, "thus" is the correct transition word as it is used to exemplify a result, which in this context is the establishment of a constitutional concept for postal regulations.
2. **Correct Answer: B** In this example, "Furthermore" is the correct transition word as the sentence builds upon the previous idea.

Sentence Structure

While it is sometimes sad to say, but the majority of students

DON'T KNOW WHAT A SENTENCE IS!

Therefore, let's start out with some basic definitions on how to analyze basic sentence structure and we will discuss the intricacies of breaking down a sentence as we continue.

Definitions

1. noun - person, place, thing, or idea
2. adjective - a word that describes a noun and must come before a noun
3. verb - action
4. adverb - describes a verb and commonly ends in "ly"
5. pronoun - a word that replaces a noun he, she, we, it, they, us, one, etc...
6. Collective Pronouns - Nouns that sound plural but are actually singular (everyone, everybody, no one, none, etc.)
7. Conjunction - words or phrases that connect independent clauses. FANBOYS - For, and, nor, but, or, yet, so
8. Sentence - a full complete thought. Can be broken down into what we refer to as "clauses"
9. Clauses - A way for us to split sentences and understand them grammatically. There are two types: Independent and Dependent.
10. Independent - Clauses that stand on their own and have their own [Subject - Verb - Predicate]
11. Subject - the main idea of a sentence, usually the first noun
12. Predicate - The explanation of what the subject is doing and a setup for the next sentence.
13. Dependent clauses - Do not stand on their own and rely on the independent. Cannot have their own subject
14. Preposition - a word that shows the relationship between a noun or pronoun and other words in a sentence. It usually indicates the position, direction, or time of an action or event. Examples of prepositions include: in, on, at, under, over, of, to, with, by, for, from, between, among, and through.
15. Punctuation - All forms of punctuation, comma (,), semi-colon (;), colon (:), quotes ("), and hyphens (-) are used to separate clauses in one way or another.
16. Article - a word that is used to specify a noun, either definite or indefinite. There are two types of articles: definite (Used to specify something in particular) and indefinite (Used to refer to anything without specificity).
17. Determiner - a word that is used before a noun to indicate the reference of the noun in terms of number, quantity, or possession. Examples of determiners include: a, an, the, my, his, her, our, their, this, that, these, and those.

*****Disclaimer!!!** These are for your review and will need to be memorized and understood as no individual problems are associated with these definitions. Instead, they are simply things you need to know to fully understand the types of problems associated with the common question types.

Constructing a Sentence

You will never be asked to construct sentences on the SAT, but if you don't know how to construct a basic sentence then there is no way you can properly correct complex ones. Let's go through some basic rules.

Example 1: I went to the store

Subject: "I" Represents the main idea of the sentence and is the first noun. The remainder of the sentence always revolves around the subject.

Verb: "went" must come after the subject and includes the action the subject is taking.

Preposition: "to" indicates the direction the noun is in this case, going.

Article: "the" in this case is specifying the predicate or where the noun is going. "the" is a definite article and is referring to a specific store.

Predicate: "store" the last part of the sentence. Technically the predicate is "went to the store" because it includes the verb, but the idea here is that it's just explaining where or what the subject is doing. This is also going to setup the next sentence.

*** This is an **Independent Clause** and considered a **Simple Sentence** since it's only one Independent clause.

Example 2: to buy milk.

Preposition: "to"

Verb: "buy"

Predicate: "buy milk"

*** This sentence does not have its own subject and therefore cannot possibly stand on its own. This is an incomplete sentence and is often considered a Sentence Fragment however, if we consider this as part of another sentence with a subject, then it would simply be considered a Dependent Clause

Rule: Complex Sentence

A sentence can also be composed of multiple clauses put together in various ways. It is possible to combine Independent and Independent or Dependent and Independent and in various orders. There are several ways to combine clauses to create more complex sentences:

1. Independent and Dependent Clauses can simply be combined
2. **Coordinating Conjunctions**: such as "and," "but," or "or," to join two independent clauses together.
3. **Punctuation** We often use varying forms of punctuation such as commas, semi-colons, and colons.

Example 3: I went to the store to buy milk.

Independent: "I went to the store"

Dependent: "to buy milk."

*** This is a complex sentence because it is composed of both an Independent and Dependent Clause

Rule: More than 2 clauses?

A sentence can also contain multiple dependent clauses and/or multiple independent clauses.

Example 4: Because I was tired, I went to bed early, but I couldn't fall asleep because it was too noisy.

This is a complex sentence that contains two dependent clauses and one independent clause.

Practice Problems

For practice with this crucial skill, identify whether each clause is independent or dependent and outline every word as either a subject, verb, predicate, article, determiner, or other various definition that we discussed throughout this chapter.

1. Although it was raining, we decided to go for a hike.

2. I ran to the store and bought some bread.

3. Because I didn't have any money, I couldn't buy the concert tickets.

4. He studied hard for the exam, but he still failed.

5. Although I enjoy reading science fiction, my favorite book is a historical novel.

6. While the team practiced diligently every day, they could not secure a victory in the final match.

7. If you study consistently for the SAT, you will likely achieve a high score, but remember to balance your preparation with relaxation.

8. Because the museum houses rare artifacts, it attracts visitors from all over the world, especially those interested in ancient history.

Commas!

The most commonly used form of punctuation in the English language is the comma, and yet the majority of students and people don't fully understand it's function and usage. It has a specific purpose and time when it can be used, otherwise if we just randomly throw around commas to use as "pauses" during speech, we are effectively guessing.
Let's first look at the formal definition of a comma:

The Comma!
The comma functions as a tool to indicate to readers a certain separation of words, phrases, or ideas in order to prevent misreading the writer's intended meaning.

Now, it's important to note that while reading aloud, you do use a pause. However, you cannot just start throwing commas in your writing to create artificial pauses so that you can create drama in your speech. As an example of this, have you ever heard a speech from President Obama or Winston Churchill?
The speech is written as,

"We, the people of the United States of America, have a duty to uphold and are fighting one common enemy."

However, the amount of pauses added for rhetorical effect to create drama and emphasis makes the speech seem like it is written like,

"We, the people, of the United States of America, have a duty, to uphold, and are, fighting, one common enemy!"

This is clearly ridiculous as you have 6 commas in one sentence. This is a clear example of comma splicing.

Comma Splicing
The improper usage of commas to separate clauses.

Thus, the real question is when do we actually use commas. In the following subsections of this chapter, you will learn all of the various ways to use commas on the SAT.

Modifiers

The second usage of commas are for separating clauses when modifying a sentence. Before we begin our discussion on dangling modifiers, it's important to understand modifiers in general:

Definition: Modifiers

Modifiers are words, phrases, or clauses that provide additional information to a sentence. They are used to modify, clarify, or emphasize a word or group of words in a sentence. The main types of modifiers are adjectives, adverbs, and prepositional phrases.

In order to truly gain a deeper understanding of modifiers, it's important to define the various types of modifiers. Let's look at each one:

Definition: Adjectives

Adjectives are modifiers that describe or modify nouns or pronouns. They can be used to indicate size, shape, color, texture, and other qualities. For example, in the sentence "The blue car drove down the street," the adjective "blue" modifies the noun "car."

Definition: Adverbs

Adverbs are modifiers that describe or modify verbs, adjectives, or other adverbs. They can be used to indicate time, place, manner, degree, and other qualities. For example, in the sentence "She sings beautifully," the adverb "beautifully" modifies the verb "sings."

Definition: Prepositional Phrases

Prepositional phrases are modifiers that consist of a preposition, its object, and any modifiers of that object. They can be used to indicate location, time, purpose, and other qualities. For example, in the sentence "The book on the shelf is mine," the prepositional phrase "on the shelf" modifies the noun "book."

Now, let's look at some common errors with modifiers:

Rule: Misplaced Modifier

A misplaced modifier is a modifier that is placed too far away from the word or group of words it is intended to modify. This can lead to confusion or ambiguity in a sentence.

Example 1: Correct the following sentence:

I ran quickly to the store.

Solution: The adverb must come before, therefore the adverb is misplaced and the sentence should read, "I quickly ran to the store."

Rule: Dangling Modifier

A dangling modifier is a modifier that does not have a clear connection to the rest of the sentence. This can make the sentence confusing or nonsensical.

Example 2: Correct the following sentence:

Running through the park, the tree suddenly appeared

Solution: In this situation, "the tree" is running through the park. To correct this error, the modifier should be connected to the correct subject in the sentence. The corrected sentence would be "Running through the park, I suddenly saw the tree."

Rule: Overuse of modifiers

Overusing modifiers can make a sentence confusing or wordy. It is important to use modifiers sparingly and only when necessary to clarify or emphasize a word or group of words in a sentence.

Example 2: Correct the following sentence:

The big, red, shiny, new car drove down the street.

Solution: In this situation, the use of multiple modifiers makes the sentence difficult to read. The sentence could be simplified to "The new car drove down the street."

*** The most common SAT problem involving modifiers is the **Dangling modifier**

Dangling Modifiers

When you start a sentence with a Dependent Clause, the Dependent must describe the subject in the Independent clause.

Let's work through some examples:

Sample Problem 1:

The cool morning air was refreshing against my skin as I moved rhythmically to the sound of my own footsteps echoing on the empty pavement.________________ Its golden rays spilling across the skyline, painting the city in hues of orange and pink. With each stride, the worries of the upcoming day seemed to fade away, replaced by a sense of clarity and peace that only a morning run could offer.

1. Which choice completes the text so that it conforms to the conventions of Standard English?

   (a) Running down the street, the sun rose over the horizon.

   (b) The sun rose over the horizon while running down the street.

   (c) Running down the street, I saw the sun rise over the horizon.

   (d) The sun rose over the horizon, and I was running down the street.

Sample Problem 2:

The tram system in many parts of the world can be vast and expansive. Stretching from one end of the city to the other, ____________________ often surprises both tourists and city residents. A tourist can easily take a tram through multiple cities.

2. Which choice completes the text so that it conforms to the conventions of Standard English?

    (a) the efficiency of Lisbon's traditional tram system

    (b) a tourist can easily take Lisbon's traditional tram system and

    (c) Lisbon's traditional tram system

    (d) the speed in which people can travel via Lisbon's traditional tram system

Practice Problems: Dangling Modifiers

Josephine Baker, born Freda Josephine Mcdonald in a small Missouri town, spent the majority of her career in Europe. In the 1920s, Baker took Paris by storm. Famed for her jaw-dropping performances, ____________________ By 1927, she was one of the most photographed women in the world.

1. Which choice completes the text so that it conforms to the conventions of Standard English?

    (a) one of her costumes consisted of 16 bananas strung onto a skirt.

    (b) her costume once consisting of 16 bananas strung onto a skirt

    (c) she once wore a costume consisting of 16 bananas strung onto a skirt.

    (d) 16 bananas strung onto a skirt once formed one of her costumes.

After graduating from high school, Tom was unsure about his future direction. He had always been interested in science, but he also had a passion for music. While he pondered his choices, ____________________ Tom's future seemed uncertain and daunting. He spent the next few months exploring different career options, talking to professionals in various fields, and contemplating his true interests.

2. Which choice completes the text so that it conforms to the conventions of Standard English?

    (a) Tom's future, which seemed uncertain,

    (b) his future, which seemed uncertain to Tom,

    (c) uncertain seemed Tom's future,

    (d) Tom felt his future seemed uncertain.

Watching the sunset from the beach, Maria couldn't help but feel a sense of peace. The day had been stressful, filled with meetings and deadlines. But now, as the sun dipped below the horizon, ____________________ The hues of orange and pink blended seamlessly, casting a warm glow over the entire beach.

3. Which choice completes the text so that it conforms to the conventions of Standard English?

    (a) the sunset made the colors in the sky breathtaking.

    (b) she found the colors in the sky breathtaking.

    (c) breathtaking were the colors in the sky.

    (d) the sky's colors, breathtaking to see.

Preparing her speech for the upcoming conference, Jane felt a mixture of excitement and anxiety. This was her first time speaking at an international event, and the topic was close to her heart. As she reviewed her notes and refined her points, ______________ She practiced several times in front of her colleagues, receiving valuable feedback that helped polish her presentation.

4. Which choice completes the text so that it conforms to the conventions of Standard English?

   (a) Jane's nerves began to settle.

   (b) as Jane prepared her speech.

   (c) her speech being prepared by Jane.

   (d) Jane's preparation for her speech.

After baking in the sun for hours, the cookies were finally ready to eat. Sarah had been experimenting with solar cooking, a sustainable method that relied completely on the sun for energy and for the baking process. ______________ Sarah was thrilled with the result.

5. Which choice completes the text so that it conforms to the conventions of Standard English?

   (a) Feeling both environmentally conscious and satisfied with her culinary skills,

   (b) The cookies, having been baked in the sun for hours by Sarah, were ready -

   (c) The sun-baked cookies, a result of Sarah's efforts, were ready.

   (d) Ready to eat, the cookies were a result of hours of solar baking by Sarah;

While hiking in the mountains, the view from the summit was breathtaking. Alex had always loved nature, and reaching the peak was a moment of triumph. ______________ Alex took a moment to appreciate the beauty around him, feeling a deep sense of connection with the wilderness.

6. Which choice completes the text so that it conforms to the conventions of Standard English?

   (a) Reaching the summit,

   (b) The view, seen by Alex as breathtaking,

   (c) Alex found the view from the summit breathtaking,

   (d) The summit's view was breathtaking to Alex,

The invention of the telephone by Alexander Graham Bell was a milestone in communication technology. Before its invention, long-distance communication was slow and unreliable. ______________ Bell's telephone allowed people to converse instantly over great distances, revolutionizing how people interacted.

7. Which choice completes the text so that it conforms to the conventions of Standard English?

   (a) Allowing people to converse instantly,

   (b) Bell's invention, allowing instant communication,

   (c) With the invention of the telephone,

   (d) The telephone, invented by Bell,

During the Renaissance, artists like Leonardo da Vinci and Michelangelo pushed the boundaries of art and science. Their work reflected a deep understanding of anatomy and perspective, creating lifelike and dynamic compositions. ____________ these artists' contributions helped lay the groundwork for modern artistic techniques and scientific illustration.

8. Which choice completes the text so that it conforms to the conventions of Standard English?
   (a) Through their understanding,
   (b) Understanding anatomy and perspective,
   (c) By pushing the boundaries,
   (d) The work of these artists,

In recent years, electric cars have gained popularity due to their environmental benefits. Unlike traditional gasoline vehicles, electric cars produce zero emissions, reducing pollution and dependence on fossil fuels. ____________ governments and manufacturers are investing heavily in the development and promotion of electric vehicles.

9. Which choice completes the text so that it conforms to the conventions of Standard English?
   (a) With zero emissions,
   (b) By producing zero emissions,
   (c) Consequently,
   (d) Electric cars,

The discovery of penicillin by Alexander Fleming in 1928 marked the beginning of modern antibiotics. This breakthrough transformed medical treatment, allowing doctors to effectively combat bacterial infections. ____________ penicillin saved countless lives and paved the way for the development of more advanced antibiotics.

10. Which choice completes the text so that it conforms to the conventions of Standard English?
   (a) As a result,
   (b) Penicillin, saving countless lives,
   (c) By combating bacterial infections,
   (d) Fleming's discovery,

Sample Problems: Solutions and Explanations

1. **Correct Answer: C** Answer choice A is incorrect becuase it is implying that the sun is running down the street. B is incorrect because the sun cannot simultaneously run down the street and rise over the horizon. D is incorrect because while the coordinating conjunction is properly used, the two independent clauses do not cohere to each other. Thus, the answer is C because I (an individual) can run down the street. The modifier is correctly describing the subject.

2. **Correct Answer: C** "Lisbon's traditional tram system" completes the sentence by providing the subject that "often surprises both tourists and city residents." The phrase correctly fits the context of the sentence, describing the tram system's impressive reach. The other options either do not fit grammatically or introduce awkward phrasing.

Commonly used words after commas

While you can use commas for many of the reasons described in the subsections and most often to separate Independent and Dependent clauses in various orders, it's important to note that there are common patterns to the SAT. Specifically, there are several commonly used words after commas to help distinguish certain answer choices. While this isn't a conventional grammar rule by any means, they are still important patterns to recognize in order to improve your score.

Dominate: Commonly used words after commas

Commas are used to create descriptive scenarios, so often you will see a dependent clause that follows a dependent clause that starts with the following words:

1. , verb
2. , which
3. , for example
4. , such as
5. , who/whom

***Remember:** Modifiers often come after the comma because they provide descriptions, therefore:

1. Must be descriptive of the subject that preceded it.
2. Can be removed from the sentence and still makes sense.

Let's work through some sample problems.

Sample Problems

Teddy hurried to his laboratory after his investigation revealed an amazingly sweet material. Luckily, nothing toxic had been used, so he started sampling the liquid in each flask he had employed that day. He had discovered ______________

1. Which choice completes the text so that it conforms to the conventions of Standard English?

   (a) saccharin, which he named for its extremely sugary taste.

   (b) saccharin which he named for its extremely sugary taste.

   (c) saccharin. Which he named for its extremely sugary taste.

   (d) saccharin; which he named for its extremely sugary taste.

With the advancements in technology, more people are relying on digital advertising than previously used paper advertising. Digital marketing is becoming an increasingly popular tool for ____________________ and creating content to reach customers and drive sales

2. Which choice completes the text so that it conforms to the conventions of Standard English?

   (a) businesses such as using social media
   (b) businesses. Such as using social media
   (c) businesses, such as using social media
   (d) businesses: such as using social media

Practice Problems: Commonly Used Words After Commas

As a renowned author, Jordan's ____________________ received numerous awards. Many critics consider him a pioneer in psychological fiction. His ability to delve into the human psyche sets his work apart from others. His work continues to captivate readers around the world, and his influence is undeniable. Jordan's latest novel is already a bestseller.

1. Which choice completes the text so that it conforms to the conventions of Standard English?

   (a) books which explore the complexities of human emotion have
   (b) books, exploring the complexities of human emotion, have
   (c) books, which explore the complexities of human emotion have,
   (d) books, which explore the complexities of human emotion, have

The committee approved the new ____________________ not decided on an implementation date. This delay is causing uncertainty among the staff. Everyone is anxious to know when the changes will take effect. The administration hopes to resolve this soon. In the meantime, employees are advised to continue with their current protocols.

2. Which choice completes the text so that it conforms to the conventions of Standard English?

   (a) policy, however, they have
   (b) policy, however; they have
   (c) policy; however, they have
   (d) policy, however they have,

Known for her groundbreaking research in marine biology, Dr. Ellis's ____________________ findings have influenced global conservation strategies. Her discoveries have shed light on the importance of preserving marine ecosystems. Her work has led to significant discoveries about coral reefs. As a result, many new policies have been implemented worldwide. Her research continues to inspire future scientists.

3. Which choice completes the text so that it conforms to the conventions of Standard English?

   (a) work, has led to significant discoveries about coral reefs. Her
   (b) work has led to significant discoveries about coral reefs: her
   (c) work has led to significant discoveries about coral reefs. Her
   (d) work has led to significant discoveries about coral reefs, her

The students, eager to learn new concepts, were ______________ They had prepared extensively for the session. Unfortunately, they will have to wait until next week to continue their studies. The delay was due to unforeseen circumstances. The students are looking forward to resuming their lessons.

4. Which choice completes the text so that it conforms to the conventions of Standard English?
   (a) disappointed when, the lecture was postponed.
   (b) disappointed, when the lecture, was postponed.
   (c) disappointed when, the lecture, was postponed.
   (d) disappointed when the lecture was postponed.

Despite the heavy ______________ held outdoors, attracted hundreds of people. You could feel the enthusiasm of the community as the main attraction was about to exhibit a popular rock group that hadn't performed in ages. The energy in the crowd was palpable. Everyone was excited to see the performance. The event was a resounding success.

5. Which choice completes the text so that it conforms to the conventions of Standard English?
   (a) rain, the event, which was
   (b) rain, the event which was
   (c) rain. The event, which was
   (d) rain, the event, which, was

The ______________ to increase the company's market share. Her strategy focuses on innovation and customer satisfaction. The new CEO brings a fresh perspective to the company. She has already implemented several new initiatives. The entire team is excited to see the results of her efforts.

6. Which choice completes the text so that it conforms to the conventions of Standard English?
   (a) CEO who was recently appointed aims
   (b) CEO, who was recently appointed, aims
   (c) CEO was recently appointed, aiming
   (d) CEO. Who was recently appointed, aims

The historical novel, set in the early 20th century, ______________ the social dynamics of the time. Readers gain a deep understanding of the era through its detailed narrative. The book has received widespread acclaim for its accuracy and storytelling. It provides insight into the challenges and triumphs of the period. Many consider it a must-read for history enthusiasts.

7. Which choice completes the text so that it conforms to the conventions of Standard English?
   (a) provides, insight into
   (b) provides insight, into
   (c) provides insight into,
   (d) provides insight into

Olivia, passionate about environmental conservation, has ______________ on sustainable living. Her efforts have inspired many others to adopt eco-friendly practices. She continues to advocate for a greener planet through her innovative ideas. Her startup has gained significant attention in the media. Olivia's dedication to the cause is unwavering.

8. Which choice corrects the improper use of commas in the sentence?
   (a) launched a startup, focused
   (b) launched, a startup focused,
   (c) launched a startup focused
   (d) launched; a startup, focused

The award-winning ____________ plans to open a new restaurant in the city next month. Anticipation is high as people are eager to experience his culinary creations. This new venture is expected to be a great success. The chef is known for his innovative dishes that combine traditional flavors with modern techniques. The restaurant will feature a diverse menu that caters to all tastes.

9. Which choice completes the text so that it conforms to the conventions of Standard English?
   (a) chef known for his innovative dishes,
   (b) chef, known for his innovative dishes plans,
   (c) chef known for his innovative dishes
   (d) chef, known for his innovative dishes,

The committee, after a long discussion and without reaching a consensus, decided to postpone the ____________ disappointed many members who were eager for a resolution. The decision was met with mixed reactions. Some felt that more time was needed to make an informed choice. Others were frustrated by the lack of progress. The committee will reconvene next month to revisit the issue.

10. Which choice completes the text so that it conforms to the conventions of Standard English?
   (a) decision, which
   (b) decision; which
   (c) decision which,
   (d) decision—which

Sample Problems: Solutions and Explanations

1. **Correct Answer: A** In this case, A is the correct answer because there must always be a comma before the word "which."
2. **Correct Answer: C** In this case C is the correct answer because there must always be a comma before the word "which."

Lists

There are many different ways to discuss and describe lists, but luckily on the SAT, there are only 5 that ever appear:

Rule: Commas in a Series

When listing three or more items in a sentence, a comma is used after each item except for the last one, which is preceded by "and" or "or."

Example 1: Correct the following sentence:

I need to buy milk eggs and bread.

Solution: You must separate each item using a comma, so the correct usage is, "I need to buy milk, eggs, and bread."

Rule: Parallelism

When listing items in a sentence, they should be written in parallel form, using the same grammatical structure.

Example 2: Correct the following sentence:

He enjoys reading, hiking, and to swim.

Solution: Each action in this case ends in the suffix "ing." Therefore the correct phrasing for this sentence is, "He enjoys reading, hiking, and swimming."

Rule: Semicolons in a series

When listing items that contain commas, semicolons can be used to separate the items.

Example 3: Correct the following sentence:

The conference will feature speakers from the United States, Canada, and Mexico, workshops on technology, marketing, and management, and networking events.

Solution: This situation is tricky, but you must understand that the list is discussing what the conference will feature. Let's breakdown the list:

1. Speakers from the United States, Canada, and Mexico
2. Workshops on technology, marketing, and management
3. Networking events

Thus, the correct way to phrase this is, "The conference will feature speakers from the United States, Canada, and Mexico; workshops on technology, marketing, and management; and networking events.

Rule: Capitalization in a list
When listing proper nouns, the first letter of each word should be capitalized.

Example 4: Correct the following sentence:

My favorite cities are Paris, tokyo, and New York.

Solution: Each proper noun must have a capital letter. Therefore, the correct phrasing for this sentence is, "My favorite cities are Paris, Tokyo, and New York."

Rule: Colons in a list
When introducing a list in a sentence, a colon can be used.

Example 5: Correct the following sentence:

I have three goals for this year. To save money, to travel more, and to learn a new skill.

Solution: The two sentences in this case can simple be combined by the use of a ":" since "to save money, to travel more, and to learn a new skill," is a list of the goals. The correct formulation of this sentence is, "I have three goals for this year: to save money, to travel more, and to learn a new skill."

Let's work through some sample problems.

Sample Problems

Example 1:

With the rise of the use of technology the use of libraries has exponentially decreased. Libraries, however, can still be very useful, especially for people that may not have access to the internet. ____________________ are free to use for everyone.

1. Which choice completes the text so that it conforms to the conventions of Standard English?

   (a) The library has a vast collection of books, magazines, newspapers, and DVDs that

   (b) The library has a vast collection of books and magazines, newspapers, and DVDs that

   (c) The library has a vast collection of books, magazines, newspapers, DVDs that

   (d) The library has a vast collection of books, magazines, newspapers and DVDs that

Example 2:

New York City has gained its title as one of the most popular cities in America. Millions of tourists come every year to check out the ____________ However, there are many other sites to see throughout New York and it is a place that attracts people throughout the world, especially throughout the holiday season.

2. Which choice completes the text so that it conforms to the conventions of Standard English?

   (a) city's museums, monuments, parks and activities.

   (b) city's museums, monuments, parks, and activities.

   (c) city's, museums, monuments, parks, and activities.

   (d) city's museums, monuments and parks and activities.

Practice Problems: Lists

Working in the legal field requires many different skills in order to succeed. Lawyers must be adept at analyzing complex information and communicating effectively. The skills required for the job ____________ Mastery of these skills is essential for providing clients with the best representation. Continuous learning and improvement are key aspects of a legal career.

1. Which choice completes the text so that it conforms to the conventions of Standard English?

   (a) include communication, problem-solving, reading comprehension, and time management.

   (b) include communication, problem-solving, reading comprehension, and time management,

   (c) include communication, problem-solving, reading comprehension and time management

   (d) include ,communication, problem-solving, reading comprehension ,and time management

Recent studies have shown a significant increase in childhood obesity in America. This could be the result of increased technology use and a decrease in healthy food options in America. To counteract this problem, schools have begun to increase the promotion of exercise to adolescents. They argue that the benefits of exercise ____________. Encouraging physical activity is seen as a crucial step in combating obesity.

2. Which choice completes the text so that it conforms to the conventions of Standard English?

   (a) include weight loss improved mood increased energy, and reduced stress

   (b) ,include weight loss, improved mood, increased energy, and reduced stress.

   (c) include weight loss ,improved mood ,increased energy, and reduced stress.

   (d) include weight loss ,improved mood ,increased energy and reduced stress.

Hobbies can be a vital tool not only to keep a person productive but to allow a person to escape and relax for a few hours to get through stressful situations. Specifically, when getting through a breakup the best advice is to keep your mind occupied with other activities. This can mean taking up a new hobby. Some popular hobbies ____________________ Engaging in these activities can provide a much-needed distraction and promote mental well-being.

3. Which choice correctly punctuates the list of topics in the sentence?

   (a) are reading writing, painting, dancing, and playing sports.
   (b) are reading, writing, painting, dancing and playing sports.
   (c) are reading, writing, painting, dancing, and playing sports.
   (d) ,are reading, writing, painting, dancing, and playing sports.

During the science fair, students showcased projects on a variety of topics: solar power efficiency, ____________________ and the effects of plastic pollution on marine life. The fair attracted a large audience, including parents and local scientists. Each project was meticulously prepared and presented with enthusiasm. The event highlighted the students' dedication to scientific inquiry.

4. Which choice completes the text so that it conforms to the conventions of Standard English?

   (a) the impact of deforestation on local ecosystems;
   (b) the impact of deforestation on local ecosystems,
   (c) the impact of deforestation, on local ecosystems,
   (d) the impact of deforestation on local ecosystems

The new diet plan recommends eating several types of foods: fruits and vegetables, ____________________ and lean proteins. Nutritionists believe that a balanced diet is essential for maintaining good health. Following these guidelines can help prevent chronic diseases. People are encouraged to make these dietary changes for long-term benefits.

5. Which choice completes the text so that it conforms to the conventions of Standard English?

   (a) whole grains;
   (b) whole grains,
   (c) whole grains
   (d) whole grains:

The coach advised the team to train regularly, eat nutritious foods, ____________________ before the championship game. These recommendations are aimed at improving performance and ensuring the players are in top condition. The team followed the coach's advice diligently. They were determined to give their best effort in the upcoming match.

6. Which choice completes the text so that it conforms to the conventions of Standard English?

   (a) and getting plenty of rest
   (b) and to get plenty of rest
   (c) and get plenty of rest
   (d) getting a lot of rest

For the final project, the professor expects students to submit a research paper, ____________________ and to participate in a group discussion. These tasks are designed to assess both individual and collaborative skills. The students have been preparing for weeks. The project is a significant part of their final grade.

7. Which choice completes the text so that it conforms to the conventions of Standard English?

   (a) create a presentation,

   (b) creating a presentation,

   (c) to create a presentation,

   (d) a presentation is created

The seminar covers several strategies to improve productivity: simplifying tasks, prioritizing goals, ____________________ These methods are proven to help individuals manage their time more effectively. Participants are encouraged to implement these strategies in their daily routines. The seminar aims to provide practical tools for personal and professional development.

8. Which choice completes the text so that it conforms to the conventions of Standard English?

   (a) and to seek feedback.

   (b) feedback should be sought.

   (c) and the seeking of feedback.

   (d) and seeking feedback.

A well-balanced diet is essential for maintaining good health and preventing chronic diseases. Nutritional experts recommend a diet that includes a variety of foods: fruits, vegetables, whole grains, lean proteins, and dairy products. Specifically, for bone health, ____________________ Proper nutrition plays a critical role in overall well-being. Adopting these dietary habits can lead to a healthier lifestyle.

9. Which choice correctly punctuates the list of foods in the sentence?

   (a) foods rich in calcium such as milk, cheese, and yogurt.

   (b) foods rich in calcium, such as milk, cheese, and yogurt.

   (c) foods rich in calcium; such as milk, cheese, and yogurt.

   (d) foods rich in calcium such as, milk, cheese, and yogurt.

When planning a community event, it is important to consider various factors: the target audience, the event location, the budget, and the schedule. For instance, ____________________ can help ensure the event's success and high attendance. Organizers must pay close attention to these details. Successful events are often the result of meticulous planning and coordination.

10. Which choice correctly punctuates the list of factors in the sentence?

   (a) choosing a central location, setting a realistic budget, and planning a convenient time;

   (b) choosing a central location; setting a realistic budget; and planning a convenient time.

   (c) choosing a central location, setting a realistic budget and planning a convenient time.

   (d) choosing a central location, setting a realistic budget, and planning a convenient time.

Sample Problems: Solutions and Explanations

1. **Correct Answer: A** In this example, "A" is the correct answer because the commas are correctly separating the items of the list.
2. **Correct Answer: B** In this example, "B" is the correct answer because the commas are correctly separating the items of the list.

Appositives

An appositive is a noun or noun phrase that renames or explains another noun or noun phrase in a sentence. It provides additional information about the noun or noun phrase, helping to clarify or emphasize its meaning. Appositives are often set off by commas, parentheses, or dashes in a sentence.

Dominate: Appositive

This is when you see two commas surrounding a word or phrase that describes the word/phrase that came right before it.
The word or phrase must follow these rules:

1. Must be descriptive of the subject that preceded it.
2. Can be removed from the sentence and still makes sense.

Let's work through some sample problems.

Sample Problems

Example 1:

Scientists have recently discovered a new planet that could resemble the chemical makeup of Earth. ______________ published an article recently outlining the similarities between the two planets and what this could mean for the future.

1. Which choice completes the text so that it conforms to the conventions of Standard English?
   (a) NASA the government agency that is responsible for this finding,
   (b) NASA- the government agency responsible for this finding
   (c) NASA; the government agency responsible for this finding,
   (d) NASA, the government agency responsible for this finding,

Example 2:

______________ quickly found success in college, due to his dedication and hard work. He quickly became known among his peers and professors as an academic superstar.

2. Which choice completes the text so that it conforms to the conventions of Standard English?
   (a) John, a bright and ambitious student,
   (b) John a bright and ambitious student,
   (c) John- a bright and ambitious student
   (d) John, a bright and ambitious student

Practice Problems: Appositives

Thomas Edison, ____________ an inventor who developed the phonograph, worked tirelessly on his creations. His contributions to technology have had a lasting impact on modern society. Edison's work ethic and innovative spirit serve as an inspiration to many. He held over 1,000 patents in his lifetime.

1. Which choice completes the text so that it conforms to the conventions of Standard English?

   (a) known to be

   (b) who was known as

   (c) known as

   (d) Correct as is

The novel "To Kill a Mockingbird," ____________ a classic of modern American literature, addresses themes of racial injustice. Written by Harper Lee, the book has won numerous awards. Its portrayal of moral and social issues has resonated with readers for decades. The novel is widely studied in schools across the country.

2. Which choice completes the text so that it conforms to the conventions of Standard English?

   (a) which is

   (b) that is

   (c) , which is,

   (d) Correct as is

Marie Curie, ____________ to discover radium, won two Nobel Prizes for her work. Her research in radioactivity has had a profound impact on science and medicine. Curie's dedication to her research was unparalleled. She overcame numerous challenges in a male-dominated field.

3. Which choice completes the text so that it conforms to the conventions of Standard English?

   (a) the first woman

   (b) was the first woman

   (c) the first woman,

   (d) having been the first woman,

The painting "Starry Night," ____________ one of Vincent Van Gogh's most famous works, is displayed at the Museum of Modern Art in New York. The artwork depicts a swirling night sky over a quiet town. Its vibrant colors and bold brushstrokes have captivated art lovers for generations. Van Gogh's unique style has left a lasting impact on the art world.

4. Which choice completes the text so that it conforms to the conventions of Standard English?

   (a) which is

   (b) that is

   (c) , one of,

   (d) which, is

Neil Armstrong, ____________ has inspired countless individuals to dream big. His historic achievement in 1969 marked a monumental moment in space exploration. Armstrong's famous words, "That's one small step for man, one giant leap for mankind," are etched in history. He demonstrated that with determination and effort, the impossible can become possible.

5. Which choice completes the text so that it conforms to the conventions of Standard English?

   (a) who was the first man walking on the moon,

   (b) the first man walking on the moon,

   (c) who the first man to walk on the moon,

   (d) the first man to walk, on the moon,

The Great Wall of China, ______________ stretches over 13,000 miles. It was built over several centuries to protect Chinese states and empires from invasions. The wall is a remarkable feat of engineering and a symbol of China's historical strength. Millions of tourists visit the Great Wall each year to marvel at its grandeur.

6. Which choice completes the text so that it conforms to the conventions of Standard English?

   (a) , which is made of,

   (b) made of stone, brick, and other materials,

   (c) made from stone, brick, and other materials

   (d) made from stone, broke, and other materials,

Mount Everest, ______________ attracts climbers from around the globe. Standing at 29,032 feet, it is the tallest mountain in the world. The climb to its summit is a challenging and dangerous endeavor. Many have succeeded, but some have lost their lives attempting the ascent.

7. Which choice completes the text so that it conforms to the conventions of Standard English?

   (a) known as the world's highest peak,

   (b) known to be the world's highest peak,

   (c) which is known as the world's highest peak,

   (d) which is known to be the world's highest peak,

Beethoven, ______________ remains influential in the world of classical music. His compositions are celebrated for their emotional depth and complexity. Despite losing his hearing, Beethoven continued to create masterpieces. His work has stood the test of time.

8. Which choice completes the text so that it conforms to the conventions of Standard English?

   (a) who was a composer,

   (b) a composer, having stood the test of time,

   (c) a composer that has stood the test of time

   (d) who was a composer who withstood the test of time,

The Rosetta Stone, ______________ a key to understanding Egyptian hieroglyphs, is housed in the British Museum. This ancient artifact was instrumental in deciphering the language of ancient Egypt. The stone features the same text in three different scripts. Its discovery opened up a wealth of knowledge about Egypt's history and culture.

9. Which choice completes the text so that it conforms to the conventions of Standard English?

   (a) which,

   (b) that is,

   (c) that, is

   (d) which is

Katherine Johnson, ______________ the trajectory for the Apollo 11 mission, was awarded the Presidential Medal of Freedom. Her calculations were crucial to the success of the first manned moon landing. Johnson's work at NASA broke barriers for women and people of color in STEM fields. She is celebrated as a pioneer and role model for future generations.

10. Which choice completes the text so that it conforms to the conventions of Standard English?

    (a) who was a mathematician
    (b) a mathematician, calculating the trajectory
    (c) the mathematician who calculated
    (d) a mathematician who calculated

Sample Problems: Solutions and Explanations

1. **Correct Answer: D** In this sentence, "the government agency that is responsible for this finding" is describing "NASA," so a comma on both sides must surround it
2. **Correct Answer: A** In this sentence, "a bright and ambitious student" describes "John," so commas must surround it on both sides

Comma Nouns/Pronouns

When two independent clauses are joined together in a sentence, they can be separated by a coordinating conjunction such as "and," "but," or "or," or they can be joined together with a semicolon (;) or a colon (:). However, they should not be separated by a comma alone.

The reason for this is that a comma is not strong enough to indicate a clear separation between two independent clauses. A comma is typically used to separate items in a list or to set off introductory phrases or clauses. When a comma is used to separate two independent clauses, it creates a comma splice, which is considered a grammatical error.

For example, consider the sentence "I went to the store, I bought some milk." This sentence contains two independent clauses separated by a comma. To correct this error, we could use a coordinating conjunction to join the two clauses: "I went to the store, and I bought some milk." Alternatively, we could use a semicolon: "I went to the store; I bought some milk."

Cheat: ,Noun/Pronoun

You cannot separate Independent Clauses with commas; therefore, you
CANNOT HAVE A NOUN OR PRONOUN AFTER A COMMA!!!
***Exceptions

1. Dangling Modifiers
2. Lists
3. Transition Words

Let's work through some sample problems.

Sample Problems

For each problem, pick the answer choice that rephrases the sentence in the correct manner.

The sunset over the ocean, ____________ was a breathtaking sight to behold. The sky was painted with hues of orange, pink, and purple. People gathered on the beach to watch the spectacular display. As the sun dipped below the horizon, the colors faded into twilight.

1. Which choice completes the text so that it conforms to the conventions of Standard English?

   (a) with its vibrant colors,
   (b) with its vibrant colors
   (c) with it's vibrant colors,
   (d) with its vibrant colors,

Joe decided to take his brand new corvette out for a test drive. He wanted to see what the car was capable of. ____________ But, he was forced to stop abruptly when he saw a police car in the near distance.

2. Which choice completes the text so that it conforms to the conventions of Standard English?

   (a) The car raced down the street and accelerating quickly.

   (b) The car raced down the street, accelerating quickly.

   (c) The car raced down the street, it was accelerating quickly.

   (d) The car raced down the street, then accelerating quickly.

Practice Problems: Noun/Pronoun

For each problem, pick the answer choice that rephrases the sentence in the correct manner.

Ms. Rachel is a nanny and decided to spend the day at the park with the kids. They were extremely energetic and excited to be outside for the first day of spring break. ____________. Then, they reluctantly sat down and ate their snacks before going home.

1. Which choice completes the text so that it conforms to the conventions of Standard English?

   (a) The children played in the park, laughing and running around.

   (b) The children played in the park and laughing and running around.

   (c) The children played in the park, they were laughing and running around.

   (d) The children played in the park, then laughing and running around.

A family is hosting a dinner party and decided to hire a private chef. They requested him to cook steak and have an assortment of vegetables plated for guests. ____________. He received many compliments for the food, everyone loved it.

2. Which choice completes the text so that it conforms to the conventions of Standard English?

   (a) The chef prepared the meal, he used fresh ingredients.

   (b) The chef prepared the meal and using fresh ingredients.

   (c) The chef prepared the meal, then using fresh ingredients.

   (d) The chef prepared the meal, using fresh ingredients.

Kate is an astronaut preparing for her first trip to space. Before going into her rocket for lift off, she stared at the sky in admiration. ________________. She smiled and entered her capsule, ready for her trip.

3. Which choice completes the text so that it conforms to the conventions of Standard English?

   (a) The stars twinkled in the night sky, then illuminating the darkness.

   (b) The stars twinkled in the night sky, they illuminated the darkness.

   (c) The stars twinkled in the night sky, illuminating the darkness.

   (d) The stars twinkled in the night sky and illuminating the darkness.

Sarah went to the library to study for her upcoming exams. She found a quiet corner and settled in with her books. ________________. After several hours of focused studying, she took a break to grab a coffee.

4. Which choice completes the text so that it conforms to the conventions of Standard English?

   (a) She studied diligently, making notes and highlighting key points.

   (b) She studied diligently and making notes and highlighting key points.

   (c) She studied diligently, she was making notes and highlighting key points.

   (d) She studied diligently, then making notes and highlighting key points.

During the team meeting, the manager outlined the goals for the upcoming quarter. The team members listened attentively and took notes. ________________. They were eager to start working on the new projects.

5. Which choice completes the text so that it conforms to the conventions of Standard English?

   (a) The manager explained each goal clearly, ensuring everyone understood.

   (b) The manager explained each goal clearly and ensuring everyone understood.

   (c) The manager explained each goal clearly, they were ensuring everyone understood.

   (d) The manager explained each goal clearly, then ensuring everyone understood.

John loves to cook and often tries new recipes. Last weekend, he decided to make a three-course meal for his friends. ________________. His friends were impressed and enjoyed the dinner thoroughly.

6. Which choice completes the text so that it conforms to the conventions of Standard English?

   (a) He prepared an appetizer, a main course, and a dessert.

   (b) He prepared an appetizer and a main course and a dessert.

   (c) He prepared an appetizer, then a main course and a dessert.

   (d) He prepared an appetizer, a main course and a dessert.

The hiking group set out early in the morning to reach the summit by noon. They brought plenty of water and snacks to keep their energy up. ______________. The view from the top was breathtaking, making the effort worthwhile.

7. Which choice completes the text so that it conforms to the conventions of Standard English?

   (a) They hiked steadily, taking short breaks along the way.

   (b) They hiked steadily and taking short breaks along the way.

   (c) They hiked steadily, they were taking short breaks along the way.

   (d) They hiked steadily, then taking short breaks along the way.

The artist spent months working on her latest painting. She used a mix of vibrant colors and intricate details. ______________. When she finally completed it, she felt a deep sense of accomplishment.

8. Which choice completes the text so that it conforms to the conventions of Standard English?

   (a) She added the finishing touches, perfecting every detail.

   (b) She added the finishing touches and perfecting every detail.

   (c) She added the finishing touches, she was perfecting every detail.

   (d) She added the finishing touches, then perfecting every detail.

The committee reviewed all the applications carefully. They were looking for candidates with strong leadership skills and community involvement. ______________. After much deliberation, they selected the final recipients.

9. Which choice completes the text so that it conforms to the conventions of Standard English?

   (a) They assessed each applicant's qualifications, checking references and achievements.

   (b) They assessed each applicant's qualifications and checking references and achievements.

   (c) They assessed each applicant's qualifications, they were checking references and achievements.

   (d) They assessed each applicant's qualifications, then checking references and achievements.

The marathon runners lined up at the starting point, ready to begin the race. They had trained for months and were eager to test their endurance. ________________. The excitement in the air was palpable as they awaited the starting signal.

10. Which choice completes the text so that it conforms to the conventions of Standard English?

    (a) They stretched and warmed up, preparing their bodies for the challenge.

    (b) They stretched and warmed up and preparing their bodies for the challenge.

    (c) They stretched and warmed up, they were preparing their bodies for the challenge.

    (d) They stretched and warmed up, then preparing their bodies for the challenge.

Sample Problems: Solutions and Explanations

1. **Correct Answer: A** The correct answer is "with its vibrant colors," because the phrase "with its vibrant colors" is a non-essential clause providing additional information about the sunset. It needs to be set off by commas to correctly separate it from the main clause. The option without the comma and the one with incorrect use of "it's" are grammatically incorrect.

2. **Correct Answer: B** In this example, the correct answer is "B" because the comma correctly separates the two verb phrases.

Semi-Colons

Semi-colons are primarily used to connect two closely related independent clauses, which are complete sentences that could stand on their own. Unlike a comma, which **CANNOT** separate two independent clauses, a semi-colon creates a stronger connection between them. The use of a semi-colon indicates that the two clauses are of equal importance and are closely related in meaning. In addition to

connecting independent clauses, semi-colons can also be used in lists to separate items that contain commas. This usage helps to avoid confusion and ambiguity when items in a list contain commas themselves.

However, the easiest way to understand the usage of semi-colons is simply to replace the semi-colon with a period and see if the two sentences work alone as complete ideas.

Cheat: Semi-Colons

Replace semi-colons(;) with periods, and make sure you have a full sentence before and after the semi-colon.

Let's work through some sample problems.

Sample Problems

The beautiful April day was showing the first signs of the end of winter. The sun was ______________________ in the trees. The grass was a lush and vibrant green, its beauty a feast for the eyes.

1. Which choice completes the text so that it conforms to the conventions of Standard English?

   (a) shining brightly; the birds were singing
   (b) shining brightly, the birds were singing
   (c) shining brightly- the birds were singing
   (d) shining brightly: the birds were singing

Danielle had finally moved to New York ready to embark on her mission to become a Broadway dancer. This has been her dream since she was a little girl. She had always been determined to make her dreams ______________________ stand in her way.

2. Which choice completes the text so that it conforms to the conventions of Standard English?

   (a) come true, nothing could
   (b) come true; nothing could
   (c) come true: nothing could
   (d) come true- nothing could

Practice Problems: Semicolons

Having been planning this trip for months in advance the morning of the trip was the most hectic. However, as the morning progressed, the family all packed into the car ______________ was palpable as they prepared for their road trip.

1. Which choice completes the text so that it conforms to the conventions of Standard English?

    (a) with enthusiasm their anticipation

    (b) with enthusiasm, their anticipation

    (c) with enthusiasm- their anticipation

    (d) with enthusiasm; their anticipation

Steven has had the worst week. His girlfriend left him, He was behind in his school work, and he was behind in his chores. The world around him seemed to be ______________ for a way to restore peace.

2. Which choice completes the text so that it conforms to the conventions of Standard English?

    (a) in chaos; he looked

    (b) in chaos he looked

    (c) in choose, he looked

    (d) in chaos: he looked

The morning sky was filled with hues of ______________ to behold. It was a peaceful view after the gloomy weather the previous week. Birds chirped happily as they welcomed the new day. The gentle breeze added to the serene atmosphere. It was a perfect start to the morning.

3. Which choice completes the text so that it conforms to the conventions of Standard English?

    (a) orange and pink it was a beautiful sight

    (b) orange and pink- it was a beautiful sight

    (c) orange and pink, it was a beautiful sight

    (d) orange and pink; it was a beautiful sight

In an effort to increase sustainability, the city council implemented several new ______________ a city-wide recycling program, incentives for businesses to reduce waste, and stricter regulations on water usage. These measures aim to create a greener and more eco-friendly city. Citizens have shown strong support for these initiatives. The council plans to introduce more policies in the future.

4. Which choice completes the text so that it conforms to the conventions of Standard English?

    (a) policies, these included

    (b) policies: these included

    (c) policies these included

    (d) policies; these included

The company launched its new ____________________ exceeded expectations in the first quarter. The innovative design and features of the product attracted many customers. The marketing campaign played a significant role in its success. Executives are optimistic about future sales.

5. Which choice completes the text so that it conforms to the conventions of Standard English?

(a) product line, sales

(b) product line. Sales

(c) product line; sales

(d) product line sales

The museum acquired a new collection of impressionist ____________________ from around the country came to view the exhibit. The pieces showcased the beauty and creativity of the impressionist movement. The exhibit was a major attraction and received rave reviews. The museum plans to host similar exhibitions in the future.

6. Which choice completes the text so that it conforms to the conventions of Standard English?

(a) paintings, visitors

(b) paintings: visitors

(c) paintings visitors

(d) paintings; visitors

The author finished writing her latest ____________________, she begins the process of editing. This novel is highly anticipated by her fans. The storyline promises to be thrilling and engaging. She has spent years researching and developing the plot.

7. Which choice completes the text so that it conforms to the conventions of Standard English?

(a) novel, now

(b) novel; now

(c) novel: now

(d) novel now

The team celebrated their victory with a grand ____________________ thrilled by the win. The players had worked hard throughout the season. Their dedication and teamwork paid off in the end. The parade was filled with cheering fans and colorful floats.

8. Which choice completes the text so that it conforms to the conventions of Standard English?

(a) parade, fans

(b) parade. Fans

(c) parade; fans

(d) parade fans

The chef prepared a special dinner for the restaurant's anniversary ____________________ delighted by the exquisite meal. The menu featured a selection of gourmet dishes. Each course was beautifully presented and full of flavor. The evening was a great success.

9. Which choice completes the text so that it conforms to the conventions of Standard English?

(a) guests, who were

(b) guests who were

(c) guests. Who were

(d) guests; who were

The scientist published her groundbreaking ______________ was highly praised by her peers. Her research provided new insights into climate change. It has the potential to influence future environmental policies. She has become a leading voice in her field.

10. Which choice completes the text so that it conforms to the conventions of Standard English?

    (a) research, which

    (b) research; which

    (c) research. Which

    (d) research which

Sample Problems: Solutions and Explanations

1. **Correct Answer: A** In this case, the correct answer is A because the semicolon is correctly separating two independent clauses.

2. **Correct Answer: B** In this case, the correct answer is B because the semicolon will separate the two independent clauses.

,Conjunctions

To be clear, there is no such grammar rule as ,Conjunctions which is one of the main reasons we didn't include this in the comma section.

The actual grammatical convention refers to how to use coordinating conjunctions, and in this specific case, we are using a comma before a coordinating conjunction. First, let's revisit coordinating conjunctions.

Coordinating conjunctions are a type of conjunction that are used to connect words, phrases, or clauses of equal importance in a sentence. They are called "coordinating" because they coordinate or join together two or more elements of equal grammatical value.

The most common coordinating conjunctions are: for, and, nor, but, or, yet, and so (also known by the acronym "FANBOYS"). These conjunctions can be used to join together two independent clauses, two nouns, two verbs, two adjectives, two adverbs, or two prepositional phrases, among other combinations.

There are two major rules before a coordinating conjunction:

Rule: , before a coordinating conjunction

1. Use a comma before the coordinating conjunction when joining two independent clauses (complete sentences) together.
2. Ensure that both sentences logically transition together. (Refer to the "Transition" Chapter 1C for a review.)

Cheat: ,Conjunctions

Replace the conjunction (, and for example) with a period, and make sure you have a full sentence before and after the period. Make sure you always have a comma before your conjunction.

Common Problem:
, and = ; = .

Let's work through some sample problems.

Sample Problems

The street performer drew a large crowd with his mesmerizing acts. People watched in awe as he performed daring stunts. The performer had a natural charisma that captivated everyone around. People crowd around the performer ______________ he magically contorts his body in ways that don't seem natural. The audience cheered and applauded at every move.

1. Which choice completes the text so that it conforms to the conventions of Standard English?

   (a) , or

   (b) , for

   (c) , and

   (d) , which

Paloma had a busy day planned and wanted to fit in some exercise. She knew that going to the gym would help her stay in shape. However, she also had family responsibilities to consider. Paloma wanted to go to the gym ______________ he had to take care of his younger brother. Balancing personal and family obligations was always a challenge for her.

2. Which choice completes the text so that it conforms to the conventions of Standard English?

   (a) , yet

   (b) , for

   (c) , and

   (d) , which

Practice Problems: Conjunctions

It was a perfect day for a walk in the park. The sun was shining brightly on the lovely spring morning ______________ the air was still cool and crisp. Families were out enjoying the weather, and children played happily. Flowers were in full bloom, adding vibrant colors to the scene. It felt like a refreshing start to the new season.

1. Which choice completes the text so that it conforms to the conventions of Standard English?

   (a) , yet

   (b) , so

   (c) , and

   (d) while

She embarked on a challenging hike early in the morning. She was tired and hungry from the long day of hiking ______________ she kept going. Determined to reach the summit, she pushed through the fatigue. The breathtaking views along the way motivated her. By the end of the hike, she felt a deep sense of accomplishment.

2. Which choice completes the text so that it conforms to the conventions of Standard English?

   (a) , and

   (b) , however,

   (c) , which

   (d) , but

Taylor was excited for the party. She had spent all week preparing her outfit and planning her arrival. The anticipation was almost too much to handle. She could not wait for it to start. Taylor was looking forward to seeing all her friends and dancing the night away.

3. What is the best way to combine the two sentences?

   (a) Taylor was excited for the party and to start would be something that she could not wait for.

   (b) Taylor was excited for the party; and could not wait for it to start.

   (c) Taylor was excited for the party, and could not wait for it to start.

   (d) Taylor was excited for the party: she could not wait for it to start.

The cat had been alone all day and was eager for some attention. The cat was meowing loudly ______________ stopped after she saw her owner come home. The owner gave the cat a warm hug and some treats. The bond between them was undeniable. The cat settled down happily for the rest of the evening.

4. Which choice completes the text so that it conforms to the conventions of Standard English?

(a) but she
(b) , and
(c) . She
(d) ; she

I was halfway to my destination when I suddenly remembered something important. After already getting to ______________ realized I left the stove and had to rush back home to turn it off. It was a frustrating and stressful situation. Once I turned off the stove, I resumed my journey. This time, I made sure everything was in order before leaving.

5. Which choice completes the text so that it conforms to the conventions of Standard English?

(a) work, and I
(b) work, I
(c) on. I
(d) on; I

The artist dedicated countless hours to perfecting her piece. The artist meticulously worked on her painting ______________ stepped back to admire her progress. The room was filled with the smell of paint and the sight of vibrant colors. Each brushstroke brought the painting closer to completion. Her passion and talent were evident in every detail.

6. Which choice completes the text so that it conforms to the conventions of Standard English?

(a) , and
(b) . She
(c) ; she
(d) but she

The scientist spent months preparing for her experiment. The scientist gathered all the data ______________ analyzed the results meticulously. Her attention to detail ensured accurate findings. The research was groundbreaking and opened up new avenues for further study. She was excited to share her discoveries with the scientific community.

7. Which choice completes the text so that it conforms to the conventions of Standard English?

(a) , and
(b) . She
(c) but she
(d) ; she

The runner dedicated himself to a strict training regimen. The runner trained for months ______________ felt ready for the marathon. His hard work and determination paid off. He approached the race with confidence. The support of his friends and family motivated him even more.

8. Which choice completes the text so that it conforms to the conventions of Standard English?

(a) ; he
(b) , and
(c) . He
(d) but he

The director had a clear vision for the movie. The director reviewed the script carefully ________________ made several crucial changes. His revisions improved the storyline and character development. The cast and crew appreciated his attention to detail. The final product was a film that received critical acclaim.

9. Which choice completes the text so that it conforms to the conventions of Standard English?

   (a) , and
   (b) ; he
   (c) . He
   (d) but he

The teacher wanted to ensure that all her students understood the task. She took her time explaining each part. The teacher explained the assignment clearly ________________ answered all the students' questions. The students felt confident and prepared. They appreciated her thoroughness and patience.

10. Which choice completes the text so that it conforms to the conventions of Standard English?

   (a) , and
   (b) . She
   (c) ; she
   (d) but she

Sample Problems: Solutions and Explanations

1. **Correct Answer: B** In this case "for" is being used as a shortened version of, "for the reason that," which correctly connects the two clauses. Also, if you place a period in between the two independent clauses, both sentences work.
2. **Correct Answer: A** In this case, the correct answer is "yet" being used as "but nevertheless" which correctly connects the two clauses

Colons

Colons are a punctuation mark used to introduce a list, an explanation, or a quotation in a sentence. The colon is often used to indicate that what follows the colon will explain, expand on, or provide an example of what was said before it.

It is important to note that a colon should only be used when the sentence before it is an independent clause that can stand alone as a complete sentence. Additionally, a colon should not be used to separate a verb from its object or subject, as this is the job of the comma.

Cheat: Colons

Replace the colon (:) with a period and make sure you have a full sentence before. However, what comes after the colon must be either a

1. **list**
2. **explanation of clarification**

Let's work through some sample problems.

Sample Problems

Preparing for the SAT requires a well-structured plan. Consistent practice and review are crucial for success. If you want to do well on the SAT you must do three ____________ practice rules, master techniques, and take many practice exams. This comprehensive approach will help you identify your strengths and weaknesses. By focusing on these areas, you can improve your overall performance.

1. Which choice completes the text so that it conforms to the conventions of Standard English?

   (a) things:

   (b) things,

   (c) things

   (d) things.

Traveling can be stressful if you are not well-prepared. It's important to make sure you have everything you need before leaving. Before you get to the airport you must make sure you have all your ____________ your passport, your boarding pass, and your credit card. This will help you avoid any last-minute hassles. Being organized will ensure a smoother travel experience.

2. Which choice completes the text so that it conforms to the conventions of Standard English?

   (a) documents

   (b) documents:

   (c) documents,

   (d) documents-

Practice Problems: Colons

Michelle worked tirelessly on the new project assigned to her. She put in countless hours of overtime to ensure its success. After working overtime on a new project for the company, Michelle finally got what she has been working ______________ a promotion to the project manager. Her dedication and hard work paid off. She was thrilled to take on her new role.

1. Which choice completes the text so that it conforms to the conventions of Standard English?

   (a) for:

   (b) for,

   (c) for

   (d) for.

Many famous quotes have stood the test of time. They continue to resonate with people across generations. As the famous writer William Faulkner ______________ "The past is not dead. In fact, it's not even past." His words remind us of the enduring influence of history. Reflecting on the past can provide valuable insights for the future.

2. Which choice completes the text so that it conforms to the conventions of Standard English?

   (a) said

   (b) said:

   (c) said,

   (d) said.

Conflicts can often bring out strong emotions in people. After a heated argument, feelings can be particularly intense. After the large dispute between Michelle and Noah, she came up to me and exclaimed, "he cares for ______________ he is the epitome of selfish. Her frustration was evident in her voice. It was clear that the disagreement had deeply affected her.

3. Which choice completes the text so that it conforms to the conventions of Standard English?

   (a) no one

   (b) no one,

   (c) no one:

   (d) no one;

Inspirational quotes can provide motivation and strength. They often offer wisdom that can help us through difficult times. As the renowned philosopher Friedrich Nietzsche ______________ "That which does not kill us makes us stronger." His words encourage resilience in the face of adversity. Many people find comfort in this powerful message.

4. Which choice completes the text so that it conforms to the conventions of Standard English?

   (a) wrote

   (b) wrote:

   (c) wrote,

   (d) wrote.

Expanding a company often involves significant strategic planning. The leadership team must consider various factors to ensure success. After discussing the merger, the CEO said, "the company needs to expand ______________ we must explore new markets. His vision for growth was clear. The team was ready to execute the new strategy.

5. Which choice completes the text so that it conforms to the conventions of Standard English?

   (a) globally

   (b) globally,

   (c) globally:

   (d) globally;

New policies can have widespread effects on an organization. It is important to communicate these changes clearly to all stakeholders. The report concluded, "The new policy will benefit everyone, ______ some may face challenges initially." The document highlighted both the advantages and potential difficulties. Overall, the policy was expected to improve the organization.

6. Which choice completes the text so that it conforms to the conventions of Standard English?
   (a) however
   (b) however,
   (c) however:
   (d) however;

Poetry often uses vivid imagery to convey deep emotions. Emily Dickinson's work is a prime example of this technique. Emily Dickinson wrote, "Hope is the thing with feathers ______ perches in the soul." Her words paint a beautiful picture of hope. This metaphor has resonated with readers for generations.

7. Which choice completes the text so that it conforms to the conventions of Standard English?
   (a) that
   (b) that,
   (c) that:
   (d) that;

Scientific experiments can reveal fascinating insights about natural phenomena. The process involves careful observation and analysis. The experiment showed, "When the temperature increases, the reaction rate ______ twice as fast." These findings were significant for the research team. They provided new directions for future studies.

8. Which choice completes the text so that it conforms to the conventions of Standard English?
   (a) becomes
   (b) becomes,
   (c) becomes:
   (d) becomes;

Mark Twain was known for his sharp wit and humor. His quotes often contain a mix of sarcasm and truth. Mark Twain famously remarked, "The reports of my death are greatly ______." His humorous response to a false report became legendary. It showcases his ability to find humor in any situation.

9. Which choice completes the text so that it conforms to the conventions of Standard English?
   (a) exaggerated
   (b) exaggerated,
   (c) exaggerated:
   (d) exaggerated;

Planning events requires attention to detail and flexibility. Unexpected changes in weather can often affect plans. The announcement stated, "The event will take place on June 5 ______ weather permitting." Organizers prepared backup plans just in case. The goal was to ensure a successful event regardless of the weather.

10. Which choice completes the text so that it conforms to the conventions of Standard English?
    (a) ,
    (b) ;
    (c) :
    (d) .

Sample Problems: Solutions and Explanations

1. **Correct Answer: A** In this case, the correct answer is A because there is a full sentence before the colon and a list after it.
2. **Correct Answer: B** In this case, the correct answer is B because there is a full sentence before the colon and a list after.

Hyphens

Similar to a colon, hyphens have various usages. However, on the SAT, there are only two variations that are used. We will skip a comprehensive discussion of the M-Dash and N-dash since the differentiation is not necessary for our purposes.

You can think of hyphen problems as either involving 2 hyphens that enclose a portion of the sentence or a single hyphen at the end of a sentence. It's important to understand the rules for both.

Cheat: Double Hyphens

Usually, a list of examples or additional phrases that are surrounded by "- -". They follow very similar rules to the Appositive:

1. Can be removed from the sentence.
2. If removed, however, the meaning of the sentence would change.

Cheat: Single Hyphens

Almost identical to a colon (:) except that what comes after the hyphen (-) must be some random detail.

Let's work through some sample problems.

Sample Problems

After months of hard work, the architecture project was finally completed. The effort put into every detail was evident. After working many hours on my architecture project it was finally finished. At the critique the presentation was well ________________ even the toughest critics were impressed. The positive feedback was a testament to the dedication and effort invested.

1. Which choice completes the text so that it conforms to the conventions of Standard English?

   (a) received-

   (b) received

   (c) received,

   (d) received:

Last week was particularly busy with preparations for an upcoming event. Emily took charge of organizing everything. Last week ________________ Emily sent out the invite list for the barbecue this weekend. The guests were excited about the gathering. Everyone looked forward to a fun and relaxing time.

2. Which choice completes the text so that it conforms to the conventions of Standard English?

   (a) I believe it was Thursday-

   (b) -I believe it was Thursday

   (c) ,I believe it was Thursday

   (d) -I believe it was Thursday-

Practice Problems: Hyphens

In life, certain values are essential for building strong relationships. Among these, a few stand out. Patience, honesty, and ______________ virtues are very important to me. These qualities help foster trust and understanding. Upholding these virtues leads to a more fulfilling life.

1. Which choice completes the text so that it conforms to the conventions of Standard English?

   (a) loyalty these-
   (b) -loyalty these
   (c) loyalty, these
   (d) loyalty-these

At the restaurant, we have a few guidelines that customers must follow. Generally, these rules are straightforward. The only exception to this ______________ is when there is a party of more than 6 people. In such cases, special arrangements need to be made. This helps us ensure a pleasant dining experience for everyone.

2. Which choice completes the text so that it conforms to the conventions of Standard English?

   (a) rule, and it is rare-
   (b) rule- and it is rare-
   (c) rule-and it is rare
   (d) -rule and it is rare-

Fashion choices can significantly enhance your appearance. Picking the right combination of clothes is key. A colorful ______________ would look amazing with those pants. It adds a touch of vibrancy and style. Experimenting with different outfits can be fun and rewarding.

3. Which choice completes the text so that it conforms to the conventions of Standard English?

   (a) -top such as the blue sweater, pink crop top, or purple tank top-
   (b) top- such as the blue sweater, pink crop top, or purple tank top-
   (c) top, such as the blue sweater, pink crop top, or purple tank top-
   (d) top- such as the blue sweater, pink crop top, or purple tank top,

Leadership involves embodying certain key traits. These traits help guide and inspire others. Courage, determination, and ______________ qualities define a true leader. Leaders who exhibit these traits earn the respect and trust of their followers. Effective leadership leads to positive outcomes and success.

4. Which choice completes the text so that it conforms to the conventions of Standard English?

   (a) empathy these-
   (b) empathy, these
   (c) -empathy these
   (d) empathy-these

Deadlines are critical in maintaining productivity and meeting goals. It's important to adhere to them strictly. The professor stated that the deadline ______________ will not be extended under any circumstances. This ensures that all students stay on track. Timely submissions are crucial for fair and efficient evaluations.

5. Which choice completes the text so that it conforms to the conventions of Standard English?

   (a) for the assignment, unfortunately-
   (b) for the assignment- unfortunately-
   (c) for the assignment-unfortunately
   (d) -for the assignment unfortunately-

Accessories can enhance the overall look of an outfit. Choosing the right pieces is essential. An intricate ____________ would complement that outfit beautifully. It adds a touch of elegance and style. Well-chosen accessories can make a significant difference in your appearance.

6. Which choice completes the text so that it conforms to the conventions of Standard English?

   (a) necklace such as the gold chain, silver pendant, or pearl strand-

   (b) necklace- such as the gold chain, silver pendant, or pearl strand-

   (c) necklace, such as the gold chain, silver pendant, or pearl strand-

   (d) necklace- such as the gold chain, silver pendant, or pearl strand,

Diligence is key to academic success. Consistent study habits lead to better understanding and retention of material. A diligent student, he ____________ studied every day to ensure he understood the material. His hard work paid off in high grades. Regular review helped him stay ahead in his classes.

7. Which choice completes the text so that it conforms to the conventions of Standard English?

   (a) therefore

   (b) therefore,

   (c) therefore:

   (d) therefore;

Managing time effectively is crucial in a professional setting. Employees must plan ahead to meet deadlines and expectations. The new policy states that employees must ____________ request time off two weeks in advance. This allows for better scheduling and coverage. It ensures that operations run smoothly.

8. Which choice completes the text so that it conforms to the conventions of Standard English?

   (a) always,

   (b) always;

   (c) always:

   (d) always

Clear instructions are essential for completing tasks efficiently. Following guidelines helps avoid confusion and delays. The instructions were clear: finish the project by Friday ____________ submit the report by Monday. This timeline ensured that all team members were on the same page. Meeting deadlines was crucial for project success.

9. Which choice completes the text so that it conforms to the conventions of Standard English?

   (a) and

   (b) and,

   (c) and:

   (d) and;

Reaching the top of the mountain was a challenging hike. The breathtaking view made it all worthwhile. She exclaimed, "The view from the top of the mountain is breathtaking ____________ it's worth the hike." Her excitement was evident in her voice. The experience left a lasting impression on her.

10. Which choice completes the text so that it conforms to the conventions of Standard English?

   (a) indeed;

   (b) indeed.

   (c) indeed:

   (d) indeed,

Sample Problems: Solutions and Explanations

1. **Correct Answer: A** In this case A is the correct answer because after the hyphen there is a detail that is not necessary for the sentence to retain meaning.
2. **Correct Answer: D** In this case, D is the correct answer because the extra detail, if in the middle of the sentence, must be surrounded by two hyphens.

Parentheses

This is another form of an appositive and essentially adds relevant detail to the passage. These are nearly identical to the ", ," scenario and you will never be asked to differentiate between the two. These questions are usually simple, just pay attention to both the parantheses and what the parantheses is referring to.

Cheat: Parentheses

Can be placed at any point throughout the sentence and can be removed without changing the meaning. What is within the parentheses must be either an:

1. **explanation**
2. **definition**

Let's work through some sample problems.

Sample Problems

Traveling can be quite stressful, especially when you have to deal with long hold times. I recently experienced this when trying to confirm my flight details. After waiting on hold for an hour ______________ she finally got to talk to the travel agent. The agent was able to quickly resolve my issues. I was relieved to have everything sorted out.

1. Which choice completes the text so that it conforms to the conventions of Standard English?

   (a) or possibly longer,
   (b) (or possibly) longer,
   (c) (or possibly longer),
   (d) , or, possibly, longer,

Our team at work often plans social events to celebrate special occasions. Last week, we decided to have a small get-together. We all decided to go out after work for Sarah's birthday ______________. The event was well-organized and everyone had a great time. It was a perfect way to unwind and enjoy each other's company.

2. Which choice completes the text so that it conforms to the conventions of Standard English?

   (a) , except for, Daniel
   (b) (except for Daniel)
   (c) - except- for Daniel
   (d) except for Daniel for he did not want to go to Sarah's birthday

Practice Problems: Parentheses

Place parentheses in the correct location in each sentence.

Success often requires a high level of perseverance. She set ambitious goals for herself and worked tirelessly. She was determined to succeed ______________. Despite numerous challenges, she never gave up. Her dedication eventually led to her achieving her dreams.

1. Which choice completes the text so that it conforms to the conventions of Standard English?

   (a) however long it took
   (b) (however) long it took
   (c) , however long it took
   (d) , and however long it took

Planning a family vacation can be quite an adventure. This year, we decided to bring our pets along. Our younger dog ________ will be coming on vacation with my family. We're excited to see how he enjoys the new environment. It's going to be a fun trip for everyone.

2. Which choice completes the text so that it conforms to the conventions of Standard English?

   (a) Kenzo

   (b) - Kenzo

   (c) (Kenzo)

   (d) (Kenzo),

Writers often use pseudonyms for various reasons. This can help maintain privacy or create a distinct identity for different genres. The woman requested ________ that she was addressed under her pseudonym. This ensured that her true identity remained confidential. It was a personal choice she valued greatly.

3. Which choice completes the text so that it conforms to the conventions of Standard English?

   (a) - actually, she pleaded

   (b) actually, (she pleaded)

   (c) (actually she pleaded)

   (d) (actually) she pleaded

In movies, characters often face dramatic dilemmas. These moments can create intense suspense. The actress exclaimed, "What should I do if he ________ comes looking for you tomorrow? Her tone was filled with urgency. The scene captured the audience's attention completely.

4. Which choice completes the text so that it conforms to the conventions of Standard English?

   (a) (the detective)

   (b) , the detective

   (c) ; the detective;

   (d) , and the detective

Philosophical ideas often provide deep insights into human nature. Ancient philosophers have greatly influenced modern thought. The ancient philosopher ________ believed that happiness is the highest good. His teachings continue to be studied and respected. Many find his perspectives still relevant today.

5. Which choice completes the text so that it conforms to the conventions of Standard English?

   (a) Aristotle

   (b) - Aristotle

   (c) (Aristotle)

   (d) (Aristotle),

Classic literature often explores complex themes. These stories remain popular across generations. My favorite novel, ________, explores themes of love and betrayal. The intricate plot and memorable characters make it a timeless read. It's a book I highly recommend to others.

6. Which choice completes the text so that it conforms to the conventions of Standard English?

   (a) Pride and Prejudice

   (b) - Pride and Prejudice

   (c) (Pride and Prejudice)

   (d) (Pride and Prejudice),

Clear communication is essential for effective meetings. Providing the correct location is particularly important. The meeting will take place in room 302 ________________ not room 304. This ensures that all participants arrive at the right place. Accurate information helps avoid confusion and delays.

7. Which choice completes the text so that it conforms to the conventions of Standard English?

   (a) (remember)

   (b) - remember

   (c) (remember),

   (d) remember

Losing personal items can be very frustrating. It often leads to a frantic search. She asked if anyone had seen her keys ________________ which she misplaced earlier. Everyone helped look around. Fortunately, they were found under a pile of papers.

8. Which choice completes the text so that it conforms to the conventions of Standard English?

   (a) (this morning)

   (b) - this morning

   (c) (this morning),

   (d) this morning

Scientific experiments often involve careful observation. The hypothesis is a crucial part of the process. The scientist hypothesized that the solution ________________ would change color when heated. This prediction was based on prior knowledge and research. Testing it would provide valuable data.

9. Which choice completes the text so that it conforms to the conventions of Standard English?

   (a) , a mixture of chemicals

   (b) (a mixture of chemicals)

   (c) - a mixture of chemicals

   (d) a mixture of chemicals

Hiking can be a wonderful way to experience nature. Each trip brings new discoveries. During the hike, we encountered a variety of wildlife ________________ including deer and rabbits. The diversity of animals added to the adventure. It was a memorable outing for everyone.

10. Which choice completes the text so that it conforms to the conventions of Standard English?

    (a) (and birds)

    (b) - and birds

    (c) , and birds

    (d) and birds

Sample Problems: Solutions and Explanations

1. **Correct Answer: C** In this example, the parentheses should be placed around "or possibly longer" because it can be removed without changing the meaning of the sentence. Answer choice A is incorrect because the point made "possibly longer" is an unnecessary description of the time in the sentence. Answer B is incorrect because if you remove the portion in parentheses, the sentence no longer follows proper verb tense consistency. D is simple comma splicing.

2. **Correct Answer: B** The parentheses should be placed around "except for Daniel" because it can be removed without changing the meaning of the sentence and adds relevant description of who attended the party. A and C are incorrect because we are creating a false appositive and when removing that phrase, the sentence no longer has logical consistency. D is incorrect because it is simply redundant

Active vs. Passive Voice

There are various forms of speech and to understand the types of speech is to have a thorough understanding of the difference between active and passive voice.

Definition: Active Voice

A form of speech when the subject performs the action. This creates a direct and clear sentence structure that is often preferred in writing.

Examples:

1. Tom wrote the essay.
2. The dog chased the cat.
3. The teacher gave the students an assignment.

In these sentences, the subject (Tom, dog, teacher) is performing the action (wrote, chased, gave). This makes the sentence clear and direct.

Definition: Passive Voice

In the passive voice, the subject receives the action. This can make the sentence structure more complicated and can sometimes make the sentence less clear.

Examples:

1. The essay was written by Tom.
2. The cat was chased by the dog.
3. The students were given an assignment by the teacher.

In these sentences, the subject (essay, cat, students) is receiving the action (written, chased, given). This makes the sentence less clear and can sometimes make it more difficult to understand.

Rule: When to Use Active and Passive Voice

Both active and passive voice can be used effectively in writing, depending on the context and purpose of the sentence.

Active voice is preferred when the subject is clear and the action is more important than the receiver.

Passive voice is preferred when the receiver is more important than the subject.

Luckily, it's not that important for our purposes to tell the difference between when it's best to use active or passive voice, rather there are certain forms of speech that call for specific tenses and words that allow for active or passive form. The two types that the SAT prefers to test students on are "Who vs. Whom" and "Affect vs. Effect." We will discuss both in the subsequent sub-chapters and easy ways to distinguish what is right and wrong.

Who/Whom

"Who" and "whom" are often confused, but they have different grammatical functions in a sentence.

Who

"Who" is used as a subject pronoun, meaning it is used to refer to the person or thing that is performing the action in a sentence.

Examples:

1. Who is coming to the party?
2. Who wrote this book?
3. Who is going to the store?

In each of these sentences, "who" is used to refer to the subject of the sentence, the person or thing that is performing the action.

Definition: Whom

"Whom" is used as an object pronoun, meaning it is used to refer to the person or thing that is receiving the action in a sentence.

Examples:

1. To whom did you give the gift?
2. Whom did you invite to the party?
3. With whom did you go to the movie?

In each of these sentences, "whom" is used to refer to the object of the sentence, the person or thing that is receiving the action.

Cheat: Who vs. Whom

To determine whether to use "who" or "whom" in a sentence, it can be helpful to rephrase the sentence as a question. If the answer to the question is "he," "she," or "they," then "who" should be used. If the answer to the question is "him," "her," or "them," then "whom" should be used.

For example:

1. Who/Whom did you give the gift to? (Rephrased as a question: Did you give the gift to him/her/them? The answer is "him/her/them," so "whom" should be used.)
2. Who/Whom did you invite to the party? (Rephrased as a question: Did you invite him/her/them to the party? The answer is "him/her/them," so "whom" should be used.)
3. Who/Whom is going to the store? (Rephrased as a question: Is he/she/they going to the store? The answer is "he/she/they," so "who" should be used.)

It is important to note that in informal speech and writing, "who" is often used instead of "whom". However, on the SAT and in formal writing, it is important to use the correct pronoun.

Let's work through some sample problems.

Sample Problems

Circle the correct word(s) in each sentence.

Our family decided to hire someone to help with the yard work. After a few interviews, we found a reliable young man. Griffen was the boy ___________ we hired to mow the lawn. He came highly recommended by our neighbors. His work has been outstanding so far.

1. Which choice completes the text so that it conforms to the conventions of Standard English?

   (a) whom

   (b) who

   (c) that

   (d) which

The class was known for its challenging exams. Many students struggled to achieve high grades. Tony was the only kid in the class ___________ scored above a B+ on the exam. His hard work and dedication paid off. He became a role model for his peers.

2. Which choice completes the text so that it conforms to the conventions of Standard English?

   (a) , and

   (b) who

   (c) whom

   (d) that

Practice Problems: Who/Whom

Circle the correct word(s) in each sentence.

Historical figures often inspire future generations. Their achievements continue to be celebrated. Alexander Hamilton was a historical role model ___________ millions of people admire. His contributions to the founding of the United States are well-documented. He remains a significant figure in American history.

1. Which choice completes the text so that it conforms to the conventions of Standard English?

   (a) whom

   (b) who

   (c) that

   (d) , which

Finding a good healthcare provider can be challenging. Recommendations from friends can be helpful. The dentist ___________ you recommended does not take my insurance. This was disappointing news. I will have to continue my search for a new dentist.

2. Which choice completes the text so that it conforms to the conventions of Standard English?

   (a) who

   (b) whom

   (c) that

   (d) , which

Friendships play a crucial role in our lives. They provide support and companionship. One of the most important things in life is having friends ________ you can depend on. These relationships are invaluable. They make life's journey more enjoyable.

3. Which choice completes the text so that it conforms to the conventions of Standard English?

   (a) who
   (b) that
   (c) whom
   (d) which

Seeking advice can be beneficial in many situations. It's important to know who to turn to. I have a question. ________ should I ask advice from? Choosing the right person can make a big difference. Their insights can help you make better decisions.

4. Which choice completes the text so that it conforms to the conventions of Standard English?

   (a) Who
   (b) From whom
   (c) From who
   (d) Delete the underlined portion

Concerts are a great way to enjoy live music. Sometimes, you might have an extra ticket to share. I don't know ________ to give the extra concert ticket to. It's always nice to invite someone who appreciates the band. Sharing the experience makes it more enjoyable.

5. Which choice completes the text so that it conforms to the conventions of Standard English?

   (a) Where
   (b) who
   (c) whom
   (d) to who

Extra credit assignments can boost a student's grade. They also encourage extra effort. The teacher gave extra credit to those ________ did the extra assignment. This incentive motivated many students. It was a great way to enhance learning.

6. Which choice completes the text so that it conforms to the conventions of Standard English?

   (a) that
   (b) in which
   (c) who
   (d) whom

Parents often give advice to help their children make wise decisions. They share their experiences to guide them. Tyler is the type of guy ________ my parents warned me about. It's important to listen to such advice. It can help avoid potential problems.

7. Which choice completes the text so that it conforms to the conventions of Standard English?

   (a) that
   (b) who
   (c) whom
   (d) which

Volunteering is a noble act that benefits the community. It helps those in need and fosters a sense of solidarity. Macy will volunteer her time to ________________ needs it most. Her selflessness is truly inspiring. Many people appreciate her efforts.

8. Which choice completes the text so that it conforms to the conventions of Standard English?

    (a) whoever

    (b) whomever

    (c) anyone that

    (d) whichever

Sometimes, people give gifts to show appreciation. This can be a thoughtful gesture. She bought a gift for someone ________________ she barely knew. The act of giving brought joy to both parties. It's the thought that counts in such situations.

9. Which choice completes the text so that it conforms to the conventions of Standard English?

    (a) that

    (b) who

    (c) whom

    (d) which

Internships provide valuable work experience. They are a great way to learn new skills. The company offers internships to anyone ________________ applies early. This encourages students to be proactive. Early applications increase the chances of securing a position.

10. Which choice completes the text so that it conforms to the conventions of Standard English?

    (a) whoever

    (b) whomever

    (c) who

    (d) which

Sample Problems: Solutions and Explanations

1. **Correct Answer: A** If we rephrase the sentence and answer it with - We hired "him" not "he" - the correct answer must be "whom" not "who." Choices C and D are "that" and "which" which refer to inanimate subjects and since the boy is alive, they cannot work.

2. **Correct Answer: B** In this example, "he" scored above a B+, not "him" scored above a B+ so the correct answer is "who" not "him." A is incorrect because a ", and" separates two independent clauses. The second part of the sentence would thus be incorrect. Choice D refers to an inanimate subject and this case, Tony is animate.

Affect vs. Effect

Many people often confuse the words "affect" and "effect" because they are pronounced similarly, but they have different meanings and uses in English grammar.

Definition: Affect

"Affect" is a verb, meaning to have an impact on something or someone. It refers to the action of producing a change or influence.

Examples: Affect

1. The rainy weather will affect the outdoor concert attendance.
2. His absence affected the outcome of the meeting.
3. The medicine may affect your appetite.

Definition: Effect

"Effect" is typically used as a noun, and it refers to the result or consequence of an action or event. It refers to what happens as a result of a change or influence.

Examples: Effect

1. The effect of the medicine was immediate.
2. The new policy had a positive effect on the company's bottom line.
3. The storm had a significant effect on the city's infrastructure.

It's important to understand the placement of these words, since no 2 nouns and no 2 verbs can be immediately next to each other in a sentence. As a summary, remember these two rules when figuring out whether to use "Affect" or "Effect."

Cheat: Affect vs. Effect

Cheat #1: AVEN This acronym stands for "Affect - Verb - Effect - Noun

Cheat #2: 2 Verbs and 2 Nouns cannot be immediately next to each other, so check the placement of the affect of effect

Let's work through some sample problems.

Sample Problems

Circle the correct word in each sentence.

Health is a crucial aspect of our lives. It is important to avoid habits that can harm our well-being. Max told his son that smoking cigarettes would negatively ______________ his lungs. His advice was meant to encourage a healthier lifestyle. It's vital to heed such warnings for long-term health.

1. Which choice completes the text so that it conforms to the conventions of Standard English?
   (a) affected
   (b) effective
   (c) affect
   (d) effect

School elections can be stressful for the candidates. The pressure to perform well is immense. The boy running for school president was worried if his campaign would be ________ His friends tried to reassure him. Ultimately, his dedication paid off.

2. Which choice completes the text so that it conforms to the conventions of Standard English?

(a) affective
(b) effective
(c) affect
(d) effect

Practice Problems: Affect/ Effect

Travel experiences can have a profound impact on one's life. Such trips can change perspectives and inspire new goals. The summer trip to Zimbabwe had a life-altering ________ on Taylor. He returned with a renewed sense of purpose. It was an unforgettable journey.

1. Which choice completes the text so that it conforms to the conventions of Standard English?

(a) effect
(b) affect
(c) changing
(d) affecting

School policies can significantly influence student behavior. The administration often updates rules to improve the school environment. When the school's new rules take ________, students will be allowed to leave the school campus during lunch. This change was welcomed by many. It provided more freedom and responsibility.

2. Which choice completes the text so that it conforms to the conventions of Standard English?

(a) affect
(b) affected
(c) effect
(d) effected

Incorporating healthy routines can improve overall well-being. Many people find morning exercises beneficial. Marina found that yoga in the morning had therapeutic ________ on her. It helped her start the day with a clear mind. The positive effects were noticeable.

3. Which choice completes the text so that it conforms to the conventions of Standard English?

(a) affects
(b) affect
(c) effect
(d) effects

The actions of today's society will shape the future. It's important to make decisions that benefit everyone. The choices this generation makes will ________ all future generations. By considering long-term consequences, we can ensure a better world. Our legacy depends on it.

4. Which choice completes the text so that it conforms to the conventions of Standard English?

(a) affect
(b) effect
(c) have effected
(d) have affected

Marketing strategies have evolved with technology. Social media plays a crucial role in modern advertising. The emergence of social media platforms has forever ________ the way companies market their product. These changes have made advertising more dynamic. Companies can now reach a broader audience.

5. Which choice completes the text so that it conforms to the conventions of Standard English?
   (a) effect
   (b) affect
   (c) affected
   (d) effected

Scientific research often uncovers important information. During her research on climate change, Sarah discovered crucial data. Sarah discovered that human activities have a significant ________ on global temperatures. This finding highlighted the need for immediate action. The implications were far-reaching.

6. Which choice completes the text so that it conforms to the conventions of Standard English?
   (a) affect
   (b) effect
   (c) affects
   (d) effects

Environmental degradation poses a serious threat to biodiversity. Immediate steps are necessary to address these issues. She noted that the rapid deforestation in tropical regions could ________ biodiversity. Protecting these ecosystems is crucial. Preserving biodiversity ensures the health of our planet.

7. Which choice completes the text so that it conforms to the conventions of Standard English?
   (a) affect
   (b) effect
   (c) affected
   (d) effected

Pollution has severe impacts on health. Urban areas are particularly affected. Moreover, the pollution in urban areas has been shown to negatively ________ human health. Measures must be taken to reduce pollution. Improving air quality can lead to better health outcomes.

8. Which choice completes the text so that it conforms to the conventions of Standard English?
   (a) affect
   (b) effect
   (c) affects
   (d) effects

Renewable energy sources are crucial for a sustainable future. Their adoption can bring numerous benefits. The introduction of renewable energy sources is expected to have a positive ________ on the environment. This shift can reduce reliance on fossil fuels. Cleaner energy options can lead to a healthier planet.

9. Which choice completes the text so that it conforms to the conventions of Standard English?
   (a) affect
   (b) effect
   (c) affects
   (d) effects

Addressing climate change requires urgent action. Reports often highlight the critical steps needed. Sarah's report emphasized that immediate action is necessary to mitigate the ______________ of climate change. Implementing these recommendations is vital. Collective efforts can make a significant difference.

10. Which choice completes the text so that it conforms to the conventions of Standard English?

    (a) affect
    (b) effect
    (c) affects
    (d) effects

Sample Problems: Solutions and Explanations

1. **Correct Answer: C** The word "negatively" is an adverb because it ends in the suffix "ly" and always must come before a verb - Affect. A is the wrong tense.
2. **Correct Answer: B** "would be" in this case is a verb and thus what follows must be a noun. Choice D is the wrong tense.

Concision

This is the easiest rule on the SAT and requires very little explanation of introduction. It's simply vital to understand that strong writers are the ones that

SAY AS MUCH AS POSSIBLE IN THE SIMPLEST WAY POSSIBLE!

Cheat: Concision

THE SHORTEST SIMPLEST ANSWER IS ALWAYS THE RIGHT ANSWER!

***As long as no rules are violated.

Let's work through some sample problems.

Sample Problems

Every morning, the couple followed a routine that had become second nature. They cherished the quiet moments together before the hustle of the day began. ______________ for over 20 years, the couple would sit together at breakfast and talk about what they have to do in the next week. Their conversations often included plans for family gatherings and trips. It was a cherished tradition that strengthened their bond.

1. Which choice completes the text so that it conforms to the conventions of Standard English?

    (a) Every Saturday on a weekly basis

    (b) On Saturdays- that is, every week-

    (c) Every Saturday

    (d) Each and every Saturday

Environmental sustainability has become a major focus for many communities. Efforts to reduce waste are being implemented worldwide. The new policy aims to reduce waste by encouraging people to ______________ reusable bags. This change is expected to significantly cut down on plastic waste. Community members are urged to support this initiative for a cleaner environment.

2. Which choice completes the text so that it conforms to the conventions of Standard English?

    (a) bring

    (b) bringing

    (c) brings

    (d) brought

Practice Problems: Concision

Paleontologists make fascinating discoveries that shed light on Earth's history. Recently, they found a remarkably well-preserved fossil. The fossil was dated back to about 430 million years ______________ based on the high amount of period-specific plant spores found in the sediment. This discovery provides valuable information about ancient ecosystems. Such findings continue to amaze and inform the scientific community.

1. Which choice completes the text so that it conforms to the conventions of Standard English?

    (a) ago. This dating of the fossil was

    (b) ago, with this being

    (c) ago: initial dating was

    (d) ago

Scientific experiments often face unexpected challenges. During a recent study, researchers encountered such a hurdle. The scientists were unable to complete the experiment they have been working on because they were unable to extract the ________ from the soil samples. This setback delayed their progress. They are now looking for alternative methods to obtain the necessary materials.

2. Which choice completes the text so that it conforms to the conventions of Standard English?

(a) necessary materials that they required

(b) minerals they needed to extract for the analysis

(c) necessary materials

(d) minerals that were necessarily needed

Communication involves more than just words. People often express their true feelings through non-verbal cues. Subtle non-verbal signals, such as facial expressions, operate on a subconscious, ________ someone's true feelings. These signals can convey honesty, discomfort, or excitement. Understanding these cues is crucial for effective communication.

3. Which choice completes the text so that it conforms to the conventions of Standard English?

(a) level, showing and implying

(b) level, showing

(c) level beyond conscious awareness, thus showing

(d) level, through this showing

Archaeological discoveries provide a glimpse into the past. Each find adds to our understanding of ancient civilizations. The discovery of the ancient manuscript was significant, revealing insights into civilizations that existed thousands of years ________. This document offered new perspectives on historical events. Such discoveries are invaluable to historians and researchers.

4. Which choice completes the text so that it conforms to the conventions of Standard English?

(a) ago. This finding provided

(b) ago, and this finding provided

(c) ago, providing

(d) ago

Excavations often lead to remarkable findings. These discoveries can rewrite history. During the excavation, researchers uncovered artifacts that were ________ more than 2,000 years old. These items provided a deeper understanding of ancient cultures. The significance of these artifacts cannot be overstated.

5. Which choice completes the text so that it conforms to the conventions of Standard English?

(a) thought to be

(b) - thought to be -

(c) , thought to be,

(d) (thought to be)

The fossil record provides crucial evidence about the history of life on Earth. Scientists meticulously study these remains to understand past ecosystems. The fossil was dated back to about 430 million years ________ based on the high amount of period-specific plant spores found in the sediment. This discovery has added to our knowledge of prehistoric life. Each fossil find is a piece of the puzzle.

6. Which choice completes the text so that it conforms to the conventions of Standard English?

(a) ago. This dating of the fossil was

(b) ago, with this being

(c) ago: initial dating was

(d) ago

Scientific research requires precise materials. Without them, experiments cannot proceed as planned. The scientists were unable to complete the experiment they have been working on because they were unable to extract the ________________ from the soil samples. This issue has set back their project timeline. They are now seeking alternative sources for the materials.

7. Which choice completes the text so that it conforms to the conventions of Standard English?

   (a) necessary materials that they required
   (b) necessary materials
   (c) minerals they needed to extract for the analysis
   (d) minerals that were necessarily needed

Understanding human interactions involves more than listening to words. Observing non-verbal communication is equally important. Subtle non-verbal signals, such as facial expressions, operate on a subconscious, ________________ someone's true feelings. These signals often reveal emotions that words cannot express. Mastering this aspect of communication enhances interpersonal relationships.

8. Which choice completes the text so that it conforms to the conventions of Standard English?

   (a) level, showing
   (b) level, showing and implying
   (c) level beyond conscious awareness, thus showing
   (d) level, through this showing

Climate change impacts various aspects of the environment. These effects are becoming increasingly apparent. The effects of climate change can be seen in the increasing frequency of natural disasters, ________________ in the rising global temperatures. Addressing these changes requires global cooperation. Immediate action is necessary to mitigate these impacts.

9. Which choice completes the text so that it conforms to the conventions of Standard English?

   (a) such as hurricanes and floods
   (b) and also
   (c) as well as
   (d) all of which result

Research is vital for raising awareness about critical issues. Sharing findings can drive public action. The research team published their findings, hoping to ________________ awareness about the critical issue. Their goal was to inform and engage the public. Increased awareness can lead to meaningful change.

10. Which choice completes the text so that it conforms to the conventions of Standard English?

   (a) rise
   (b) raising
   (c) risen
   (d) raise

Sample Problems: Solutions and Explanations

1. **Correct Answer: C** C is the correct answer because it is the shortest and simplest answer without violating any rules.
2. **Correct Answer: A** The sentence requires the base form of the verb "bring" to follow the phrase "to," making "bring" the correct choice. This aligns with the infinitive verb form used to express purpose.

Pronouns

Pronouns are used to replace nouns in a sentence, which helps to avoid repetition and make the language more concise and efficient. Pronouns can refer to people, animals, things, and abstract concepts, and they can also indicate gender, number, and case.

Here is a list of all the possible pronouns in English, divided by category:

Rule: Pronouns			
Personal Pronouns First Person Singular: I, me Second Person Singular: you Third Person Singular (Masculine): he, him Third Person Singular (Feminine): she, her Third Person Singular (Neutral): it First Person Plural: we, us Second Person Plural: you Third Person Plural: they, them	**Possessive Pronouns:** First Person Singular: my, mine Second Person Singular: your, yours Third Person Singular (Masculine): his Third Person Singular (Feminine): her, hers Third Person Singular (Neutral): its First Person Plural: our, ours Second Person Plural: your, yours Third Person Plural: their, theirs	**Reflexive Pronouns:** First Person Singular: myself Second Person Singular: yourself Third Person Singular: himself, herself, itself First Person Plural: ourselves Second Person Plural: yourselves Third Person Plural: themselves	**Demonstrative Pronouns:** This, that, these, those
Interrogative Pronouns: Who, whom, whose, what, which	**Indefinite Pronouns:** All, another, any, anybody, anyone, anything, both, each, either, everybody, everyone, everything, few, many, neither, nobody, no one, nothing, one, other, several, some, somebody, someone, something, such	**Relative Pronouns:** Who, whom, whose, that, which	**Collective Pronouns:** These pronouns refer to a group of people or things as a single entity. Examples: The team celebrated their victory. ("Team" is a collective noun, and "their" is the collective pronoun that refers to the group as a whole.) The audience gave its full attention to the performance. ("Audience" is a collective noun, and "its" is the collective pronoun that refers to the group as a whole.)

Replace a Pronoun with the Noun

Luckily for us, we don't have to know the rule involving every pronoun and its proper usage as that is outside the scope of the SAT. However, what is important is a general understanding of pronoun usage and the fact that it simply replaces a noun. That being said, you must make sure that the correct pronoun is being used to describe the subject in question. An easy way to do this is to simply get rid of the pronoun entirely and input the noun in question and make sure the sentence makes logical sense. While this will make the sentence redundant, it will eliminate the possibility of you using the incorrect pronoun.

Cheat: Pronouns
Replace the pronoun with the noun and check to make sure it makes sense.

Let's work through some sample problems.

Sample Problems

The factory operates efficiently thanks to the skilled workers and advanced machinery. Each machine has a designated operator. It is ________________ who is responsible for operating the machine. Their expertise ensures smooth production processes. Regular maintenance is also crucial to avoid breakdowns.

1. Which choice completes the text so that it conforms to the conventions of Standard English?
   (a) he
   (b) for
   (c) them
   (d) it

After reviewing the case, the jury deliberated for hours. They examined the evidence and discussed various aspects of the testimony. ________________ has come to different conclusions. The judge will have to consider their individual opinions. This decision will impact the final verdict.

2. Which choice completes the text so that it conforms to the conventions of Standard English?
   (a) One of the people
   (b) All of the people
   (c) The few people
   (d) Everyone

Practice Problems: Pronouns

At the meeting, various perspectives were shared on the new policy. Some participants had strong opinions. ________________ more than anyone knows what the problem is with the way she was behaving. Their insights helped clarify the situation. A resolution was reached by the end of the discussion.

1. Which choice completes the text so that it conforms to the conventions of Standard English?
   (a) They
   (b) Jack and Ryan
   (c) The people
   (d) You

The group of friends often talked about their future plans. During a recent conversation, they discussed family life. ______________ of the girls is planning on having kids anytime soon. Instead, they are focusing on their careers. They all agreed to support each other's decisions.

2. Which choice completes the text so that it conforms to the conventions of Standard English?

   (a) Neither

   (b) None

   (c) Both

   (d) She

During the sports competition, fair play is emphasized. Each team member must follow the rules. ______________ will get in trouble if our team decides to cheat. The coach constantly reminds them of this. Maintaining integrity is crucial for the team's reputation.

3. Which choice completes the text so that it conforms to the conventions of Standard English?

   (a) We

   (b) Us

   (c) Them

   (d) They

The upcoming election has everyone talking. There are several candidates, but one stands out. Nicole is the only candidate in this election who is worthy of our votes and ______________ will hopefully win the election. Her policies resonate with many voters. She has been campaigning tirelessly.

4. Which choice completes the text so that it conforms to the conventions of Standard English?

   (a) they

   (b) she

   (c) her

   (d) it

After a long practice session, the athletes look forward to their cooldown. This routine helps prevent injuries. ______________ of the athletes gets to take an ice bath after practice. They find it very refreshing. It's a vital part of their recovery process.

5. Which choice completes the text so that it conforms to the conventions of Standard English?

   (a) Each

   (b) All

   (c) They are of

   (d) However, if one

Excellent service at a restaurant can make a huge difference in the dining experience. Customers often return because of the service quality. ______________ is responsible for the excellent service at the restaurant. They always ensure that guests feel welcome. Their dedication is commendable.

6. Which choice completes the text so that it conforms to the conventions of Standard English?

   (a) He

   (b) She

   (c) It

   (d) They

The students have been eagerly anticipating their field trip. They've been planning it for weeks. The students, along with their teacher, ______________ excited about the upcoming field trip. They can't wait to explore new places and learn new things. The trip promises to be educational and fun.

7. Which choice completes the text so that it conforms to the conventions of Standard English?

    (a) are

    (b) is

    (c) was

    (d) were

Each member of the club has a designated space. They appreciate having a place to store their belongings. Each of the members ______________ their own locker. This system helps keep things organized. It also provides a sense of ownership.

8. Which choice completes the text so that it conforms to the conventions of Standard English?

    (a) has

    (b) have

    (c) had

    (d) having

The committee met several times to discuss the proposal. They had to weigh various options. The committee ______________ to make a decision by the end of the week. Their decision will impact the entire organization. It's a responsibility they take seriously.

9. Which choice completes the text so that it conforms to the conventions of Standard English?

    (a) expect

    (b) expects

    (c) expecting

    (d) expected

During the meeting, various suggestions were made. The committee considered each one carefully. ______________ of the suggestions were considered during the meeting. They wanted to ensure that all viewpoints were heard. This thorough approach will help them make a well-informed decision.

10. Which choice completes the text so that it conforms to the conventions of Standard English?

    (a) Many

    (b) Much

    (c) None

    (d) Few

Sample Problems: Solutions and Explanations

1. **Correct Answer: A** If we replace he with a noun, such as "Jon" the sentence would make complete logical sense as Jon is responsible for operating the machine. B is a conjunction and doesn't belong. C is plural and doesn't work with the verb is - refer to the verb tense consistency chapter in Chapter 16 to find out more. D is referring to an object and an object cannot operate a machine.

2. **Correct Answer: D** The verb in the sentence is "has" thus, "everyone has" is correct because everyone is a collecting pronoun and thus acts singular. B and C are incorrect because they are plural. A is incorrect because while it is fully singular, One of the people is a logical fallacy.

I vs. Me

One common grammar issue that often arises on the grammar portion of the SAT is the misuse of the pronouns "I" and "me." In short, "I" is a subject pronoun, while "me" is an object pronoun.

Definition: Subject Pronoun "I"

A subject pronoun is used as the subject of a sentence or clause, meaning that it is performing the action of the sentence. For example, "I went to the store" or "She and I are going to the park." In these sentences, "I" is the subject, because it is performing the action of going to the store or going to the park.

Definition: Object Pronoun "Me"

An object pronoun is used as the object of a verb or preposition, meaning that it is the recipient of the action. For example, "She gave the book to me" or "He invited her and me to the party." In these sentences, "me" is the object, because it is the recipient of the book or the invitation.

Luckily, there is an easy way to determine whether to use "I" or "me."

Cheat: I vs. Me

Remove the other person or persons from the sentence and see if "I" or "me" still makes sense.

For example, in the sentence "She and I went to the store," if we remove "she," we get "I went to the store," which is correct. In the sentence "He invited her and me to the party," if we remove "her," we get "He invited me to the party," which is also correct.

Let's work through some sample problems.

Sample Problems

Every weekend, my friends and I like to hang out. Sometimes we go hiking, other times we play video games. This weekend, ______________ are going to the movies. It's always fun when we get together. We can't wait to see the new blockbuster film.

1. Which choice completes the text so that it conforms to the conventions of Standard English?
   (a) Bob and I
   (b) Bob and me
   (c) Me and Bob
   (d) Bob

During the school assembly, awards were handed out to outstanding students. The teacher was proud of all the achievements. The teacher gave the award to ______________. The entire class cheered for the winners. It was a memorable moment for everyone.

2. Which choice completes the text so that it conforms to the conventions of Standard English?
   (a) my friend and I
   (b) my friends and I
   (c) my friend and me
   (d) both of my friends and I

Practice Problems: I vs. Me

Moving day can be quite stressful. Sarah needed help with all her heavy furniture. Sarah asked ________________ to help her move. We gladly agreed to assist her. By the end of the day, everything was in place.

1. Which choice completes the text so that it conforms to the conventions of Standard English?

    (a) Joe and me

    (b) I and Joe

    (c) Joe and I

    (d) Joe and it

Friendships can sometimes face challenges. Recently, there was a misunderstanding. There was a great deal of tension between ________________. They needed to have an honest conversation. Thankfully, they resolved their issues.

2. Which choice completes the text so that it conforms to the conventions of Standard English?

    (a) my friend and I

    (b) my friend and me

    (c) they

    (d) there

Customer service is important in any business. If you have any questions, please reach out to Carl or ________________. They are always ready to help. Providing good support ensures customer satisfaction.

3. Which choice completes the text so that it conforms to the conventions of Standard English?

    (a) myself

    (b) he

    (c) him

    (d) me

Company policies can significantly impact employees. The new policy will affect both the employees and ________________. Understanding these changes is crucial for everyone. The management has scheduled a meeting to discuss the details.

4. Which choice completes the text so that it conforms to the conventions of Standard English?

    (a) I

    (b) us

    (c) they

    (d) them

Collaboration on projects can be very rewarding. The report was prepared by Julia and ________________. They worked hard to ensure it was thorough and accurate. Their teamwork paid off in the end.

5. Which choice completes the text so that it conforms to the conventions of Standard English?

    (a) I

    (b) me

    (c) she

    (d) her

Confidential conversations can sometimes reveal important insights. Between you and ________________, I think this project is going to fail. It's important to discuss our concerns openly. This way, we can find a solution before it's too late.

6. Which choice completes the text so that it conforms to the conventions of Standard English?

(a) I

(b) me

(c) he

(d) him

New procedures were introduced at the office. ________________ should be aware of the new procedures. This ensures that everyone follows the same guidelines. Adherence to these procedures is crucial for smooth operations.

7. Which choice completes the text so that it conforms to the conventions of Standard English?

(a) Everyone

(b) Each of them

(c) Him

(d) Her

Teamwork is essential for success. The success of the team depends on you and ________________. Working together, we can achieve great things. Let's focus on our common goals.

8. Which choice completes the text so that it conforms to the conventions of Standard English?

(a) I

(b) us

(c) me

(d) he

The new assignment has been distributed. Each of the students ________________ expected to complete the assignment on time. This will help them stay on track with the curriculum. Timely submission is important for their grades.

9. Which choice completes the text so that it conforms to the conventions of Standard English?

(a) is

(b) are

(c) were

(d) was

Errors in the project were identified. Neither the manager nor the employees ________________ responsible for the error. It was a system fault. Addressing this issue is a priority.

10. Which choice completes the text so that it conforms to the conventions of Standard English?

(a) is

(b) are

(c) was

(d) were

Sample Problems: Solutions and Explanations

1. **Correct Answer: A** If you remove the "Bob and" the sentence reads "I are going to the movies." We obviously have to change the verb to reflect the fact that it's only on person, thus it finally becomes "I am going to the movies." You cannot start the sentence with "Me," so B and C is incorrect. D makes no logical sense.

2. **Correct Answer: C** if you remove the "my friend and" the sentence reads, "The teacher gave the award to me." This is correct. You cannot say, "The teacher gave the award to I" so A and B are incorrect. D is simply too long and redundant.

Tenses

Verbs are an essential part of English grammar, and they indicate the time frame of an action. Verb tenses can be used to express actions in the past, present, or future, and it is important to understand how they work to communicate effectively. In this chapter, we will explore the various forms of past, present, future, singular and plural tenses and how they apply on the SAT.

Past-Present-Future

We are going to start our discussion of tenses by delving into past-present-future tenses.

Definition: Past Tense

The past tense is used to describe actions that have already happened.
There are four main forms of the past tense in English: simple past, past progressive, past perfect, and past perfect progressive.

Rule: Simple Past

This is the most basic form of the past tense, and it is used to describe actions that happened at a specific time in the past.

Examples:

1. Yesterday, I went to the store.
2. She studied for hours last night.
3. They played soccer all afternoon.

Rule: Past Progressive:

This tense is used to describe actions that were in progress at a specific time in the past.

Examples:

1. While I was driving, it started to rain.
2. She was studying when the power went out.
3. They were playing soccer when the storm hit.

Rule: Past Perfect

This tense is used to describe actions that were completed before another action in the past.

Examples:

1. He had already eaten dinner before we arrived.
2. She had finished her homework before her friends came over.
3. They had left the party before we got there.

Rule: Past Perfect Progressive

This tense is used to describe actions that were in progress before another action in the past.

Examples:

1. She had been working for six hours when her boss called her into his office.
2. They had been driving for three hours before they reached their destination.
3. He had been studying for weeks before the final exam.

Now, let's look into present tenses:

Definition: Present Tense

The present tense is used to describe actions that are happening now or regularly. There are four main forms of the present tense in English: simple present, present progressive, present perfect, and present perfect progressive.

Rule: Simple Present

This is the most basic form of the present tense, and it is used to describe actions that happen regularly or are true in general.

Examples:

1. I eat breakfast every day.
2. She speaks three languages fluently.
3. They love to travel.

Rule: Present Progressive

This tense is used to describe actions that are happening right now.

Examples:

1. I am writing a book.
2. She is cooking dinner.
3. They are watching a movie.

Rule: Present Perfect

This tense is used to describe actions that started in the past and continue up to the present.

Examples:

1. I have lived in this city for five years.
2. She has worked at the company since 2010.
3. They have known each other since childhood.

Rule: Present Perfect Progressive

This tense is used to describe actions that started in the past and continue up to the present, emphasizing the duration of the action.

Examples:

1. She has been working on the project for two weeks.
2. They have been studying for the exam all day.
3. I have been waiting for an hour.

Definition: Future Tense

The future tense is used to describe actions that will happen in the future. There are four main forms of the future tense in English: simple future, future progressive, future perfect, and future perfect progressive.

Rule: Simple Future

This is the most basic form of the future tense, and it is used to describe actions that will happen in the future.

Examples:

1. I will visit my parents next weekend.
2. She will start her new job on Monday.
3. They will travel to Europe next year.

Verb-Tense Consistency

These problems are very similar to Pronoun issues and while we considered putting them into the same Chapter, they don't have to only be related to pronouns but the nouns themselves.

This concept is quite important as every subject must come before a verb. This is what makes the basic tenets of an Independent Clause - **Subject-Verb Agreement**

The rules, however, are simple:

Cheat: Verb-Tense Consistency	
Singular Nouns Must have Plural Verbs!	**Plural Nouns** Must have singular Verbs!

***This does not apply to helper verbs and personal pronouns, such as I, they, is, are, has, and have.

Let's work through some sample problems.

Sample Problems

Tommy and his sister love spending time together. After finishing their homework, they always find fun activities to do. Today, Tommy and his sister ________________ going to get ice cream. They can't wait to choose their favorite flavors. It's their special treat for a job well done.

1. Which choice completes the text so that it conforms to the conventions of Standard English?

   (a) is
   (b) are
   (c) will
   (d) would be

My staff takes great pride in their work. They are dedicated to meeting client needs and improving our services. My staff ________________ in providing better service than competing firms. Their commitment to excellence sets us apart. We continually strive for customer satisfaction.

2. Which choice completes the text so that it conforms to the conventions of Standard English?

   (a) believes
   (b) believe
   (c) belief
   (d) beliefs

Practice Problems: Verb-Tense Consistency

Making decisions can be challenging. Before finalizing your choice, it's essential to consider all relevant information. Here ________________ two more factors to consider before making your decision. Weighing all the options can lead to better outcomes. Take your time to evaluate everything thoroughly.

1. Which choice completes the text so that it conforms to the conventions of Standard English?

   (a) is
   (b) are
   (c) may be
   (d) would be

Traveling can be full of unexpected challenges. Despite these obstacles, determination is key. Neither the rain nor the darkness ________ going to stop me from getting to our destination on time. Perseverance always pays off. Let's keep pushing forward.

2. Which choice completes the text so that it conforms to the conventions of Standard English?

   (a) is

   (b) or

   (c) are

   (d) will

Community involvement is crucial for societal improvement. Recently, there's been a focus on safety measures. A majority of the community ________ implementing new laws to decrease drinking and driving. This collective effort aims to save lives. Together, we can make a difference.

3. Which choice completes the text so that it conforms to the conventions of Standard English?

   (a) support

   (b) will have supported

   (c) supports

   (d) would be supporting

Vacations are a wonderful time to relax and bond with family. This year, we've planned an exciting trip. My whole family ________ vacationing in Mexico this winter break. We'll explore new places and create unforgettable memories. Everyone is looking forward to the adventure.

4. Which choice completes the text so that it conforms to the conventions of Standard English?

   (a) is

   (b) will

   (c) is going to be

   (d) are

College life comes with its own set of challenges. Stress management is essential for success. One in three stressed college students ________ with skipping classes and sleeping in. Finding healthy coping mechanisms is important. Let's support each other in managing stress.

5. Which choice completes the text so that it conforms to the conventions of Standard English?

   (a) cope

   (b) coped

   (c) is coping

   (d) copes

Higher education requires dedication and time. Four years ________ considered the normal amount of time to earn a college degree. This period allows for comprehensive learning and personal growth. Many students find this journey rewarding. It sets the foundation for their future careers.

6. Which choice completes the text so that it conforms to the conventions of Standard English?

   (a) may or may not be

   (b) can

   (c) is

   (d) will

Music concerts are popular social events. People gather to enjoy live performances. There ________ lots of people showing up for the concert. The atmosphere is always electric. Fans are eager to see their favorite artists perform.

7. Which choice completes the text so that it conforms to the conventions of Standard English?
   (a) is
   (b) are
   (c) their
   (d) , and

Research findings are often anticipated eagerly. They provide insights into various subjects. The results of the survey ________ published next week. Everyone is curious about the conclusions. This information could lead to significant developments.

8. Which choice completes the text so that it conforms to the conventions of Standard English?
   (a) will be
   (b) are
   (c) has been
   (d) were

School plays require a lot of preparation. The teacher oversees all the activities. The teacher, along with the students, ________ preparing for the school play. Rehearsals are held daily. Everyone is excited for the upcoming performance.

9. Which choice completes the text so that it conforms to the conventions of Standard English?
   (a) are
   (b) were
   (c) was
   (d) is

Workshops are great opportunities for learning new skills. Participation certificates are often given at the end. Each of the participants ________ given a certificate at the end of the workshop. This recognition motivates them to keep learning. They proudly display these certificates.

10. Which choice completes the text so that it conforms to the conventions of Standard English?
   (a) were
   (b) was
   (c) are
   (d) is

Sample Problems: Solutions and Explanations

1. **Correct Answer: B** Tommy and his sister are two people, therefore, the helper verb associated must be are. A is singular. C and D are not the correct verbs for this sentence.
2. **Correct Answer: A** The subject here is "My staff", which is singular. Therefore, the verb must be plural. C and D are nouns and not verbs.

False Comparison

When comparing two or more nouns, verbs, or anything for that matter, they must be comparable. What that means essentially is the fact that you must compare things that can actually be compared. In other words, you cannot compare a calculator with the subject of mathematics. It's impossible because a calculator is an object and the subject of mathematics is a subject matter and have entirely different functions and descriptions. In the English language, this may get trick at times, but there are easy and effective methods to ensure

Cheat: False Comparison

When comparing two or more things, they must be in the same classification and type. In other words, we can compare an animal to an animal or a size to a size, but we cannot compare size to an animal.

The most common problem that appears on the exam is issues with the word, **"Than!"**

Often, you will find a specific problem involving a false comparison of the word "than" and it will compare an object with an object, so be cautious of a phrase such as "than that of." It will be easier to explain through an example, so work through the next 2 sample problems before you try any problems on your own.

Let's work through some sample problems.

Sample Problems

Elephants are known for their massive size. Their physical features are quite distinct from those of smaller animals. The size of the elephant is bigger ________________ the mouse. This comparison highlights the vast difference between the two creatures. It's fascinating to observe such contrasts in the animal kingdom.

1. Which choice completes the text so that it conforms to the conventions of Standard English?

   (a) than

   (b) then

   (c) from

   (d) than that of

Academic performance is often compared among siblings. John and his brother have always been competitive. John's grades are better ________________ his brother's. This achievement makes John proud and motivates his brother to work harder. Healthy competition can lead to great results.

2. Which choice completes the text so that it conforms to the conventions of Standard English?

   (a) than

   (b) than that of

   (c) then

   (d) from

Practice Problems:

Circle the correct phrase in each sentence.

Financial stability is crucial for a comfortable life. Over the years, I've learned to manage my finances well. I had more money now ________________ ever before. This financial freedom allows me to pursue my passions. It's a rewarding feeling.

1. Which choice completes the text so that it conforms to the conventions of Standard English?

   (a) then

   (b) than

   (c) then I had

   (d) Delete the underlined portion

Nature offers breathtaking views that are often unparalleled. The sky and the sea present such beauty. The color of the sky is more beautiful ________________ the sea. Observing these natural wonders brings a sense of peace. It's a reminder of the world's beauty.

2. Which choice completes the text so that it conforms to the conventions of Standard English?

   (a) then

   (b) than

   (c) than that of

   (d) than the color of

My day was filled with various activities. I first went to the park ________________ went home. It was a refreshing break from my usual routine. Spending time outdoors always recharges me. I ended the day feeling rejuvenated.

3. Which choice completes the text so that it conforms to the conventions of Standard English?

   (a) then

   (b) than

   (c) than that of

   (d) next

School populations can vary greatly. This affects the resources and opportunities available. There are more students in Lincoln High School ________________ Madison High School. This difference impacts class sizes and extracurricular activities. Each school has its unique strengths.

4. Which choice completes the text so that it conforms to the conventions of Standard English?

   (a) then

   (b) than

   (c) than that

   (d) than there are in

Personal belongings can hold significant sentimental value. Among my possessions, some items are particularly special. The book on the table belongs to ________________. It's one of my favorite books. I always enjoy re-reading it.

5. Which choice completes the text so that it conforms to the conventions of Standard English?

   (a) I

   (b) me

   (c) my

   (d) mine

Companies continuously seek ways to improve. Implementing new strategies can lead to significant benefits. The company decided to implement the new policy ________ improve productivity. This change is expected to yield positive results. Employees are adapting well to the new system.

6. Which choice completes the text so that it conforms to the conventions of Standard English?
   (a) in order to
   (b) in order
   (c) so that
   (d) for to

Problem-solving is a crucial skill in any field. Finding the right solution can be challenging. Neither of the solutions ________ the problem effectively. This requires further analysis and brainstorming. Persistence will eventually lead to success.

7. Which choice completes the text so that it conforms to the conventions of Standard English?
   (a) solve
   (b) solves
   (c) solving
   (d) solved

Application reviews are essential for selecting the right candidates. The process involves careful consideration of each applicant. The committee ________ reviewing the applications now. This ensures a fair and thorough selection process. Candidates will be notified of the results soon.

8. Which choice completes the text so that it conforms to the conventions of Standard English?
   (a) are
   (b) is
   (c) was
   (d) were

Travel plans can be exciting and challenging. Deciding on the destinations requires careful thought. She wanted to travel to France ________ Italy. Each country offers unique experiences. It's a tough choice to make.

9. Which choice completes the text so that it conforms to the conventions of Standard English?
   (a) or
   (b) and
   (c) nor
   (d) but

Science lectures can be very enlightening. Clear explanations help the audience understand complex concepts. The scientist explained the phenomenon clearly ________ the audience. This enhanced their comprehension of the subject. Everyone left the lecture feeling more informed.

10. Which choice completes the text so that it conforms to the conventions of Standard English?
    (a) to
    (b) for
    (c) with
    (d) at

Sample Problems: Solutions and Explanations

1. **Correct Answer: D** This is a false comparison because we are comparing the size of the elephant, in this case we can say 1000kg to an animal which is the mouse. Since you cannot compare size with an animal, this is incorrect. If you look at this example, you will realize that we are now comparing size with the word *that. that* is a pronoun and allows us to replace the word "size." Now if you really think about the reading of the sentence, the reading of the sentence fully and completely is:

   The size of the elephant is bigger than the size of the mouse.

   The reason we don't say "size" twice is because that would make the sentence redundant. Choice B is incorrect because "then" refers to a sequence of events. C is incorrect because it is location.

2. **Correct Answer: B** This is a false comparison because we are comparing John's brother's grades to John's grades. If we pick answer choice A, we are comparing John's grades with his brother and not his brother's grades. It's like comparing an A with a person - not possible! If we replace "that" with the actual noun which is grades, the actual sentence becomes, "John's grades are better that the grades of his brother's." Choice A is a false comparison, C is a sequence of events, and D is referring to a location.

Apostrophe

Apostrophes (') are used for contractions, singular possession, or plural possession. Each usage is important to understand and practice, but relatively simple to master once you understand the rules.

Rule: Contractions	Rule: Singular Possession	Rule: Plural Possession
Two words combined together They're = They are Couldn't = Could not It's color	A singular noun can possess something if followed by 's. Jon's car	A plural noun can possess something if followed by s'. The only exception to this is for a name that already ends in s. The two actresses' roles

There is a very interesting and cool rule when it comes to possession:

Cheat: Possession

For singular possession, replace the "'s" with his, her, or its - indicating singular possession.
For plural possession, replace the "s'" with their or our - checking plural possession.

Let's work through some sample problems.

Sample Problems

Those stunning costumes, elaborately designed with intricate details and vibrant colors, look amazing on them. Each costume appears to be custom-made, perfectly fitting the contours of the _______________ bodies, enhancing their overall appearance on stage. The rich fabric and ornate decorations reflect a high level of craftsmanship and attention to detail, making them truly stand out. The way the costumes complement the lighting and set design adds to the overall visual impact of the performance. Every element of the costumes contributes to bringing the characters to life in a spectacular way.

1. Which choice completes the text so that it conforms to the conventions of Standard English?

   (a) actresses

   (b) actress's

   (c) actresses's

   (d) actresses'

The _______________ hat, a distinctive part of his uniform, flew off into the water because of the strong wind that suddenly picked up speed. As the wind gusted through the harbor, it caught the brim of his hat, lifting it high into the air before dropping it into the choppy waves. The sailor, realizing what had happened, quickly ran to the edge of the dock, but it was too late. The hat bobbed in the water, drifting away from the dock with each passing second. It was a moment of both surprise and frustration as he watched his hat float out of reach.

2. Which choice completes the text so that it conforms to the conventions of Standard English?

   (a) sailors

   (b) sailor

   (c) sailor's

   (d) sailors'

Practice Problems

________ it seem strange that we have not heard back from Carol regarding the budget yet? Her input is usually prompt, and she never misses an important deadline. This delay is unusual and has left everyone concerned about the progress of the project. We were expecting her feedback by the end of last week, but there has been no communication from her side. It is crucial that we get her response soon to move forward with the financial planning.

1. Which choice completes the text so that it conforms to the conventions of Standard English?

   (a) Doesnt

   (b) Doesn't

   (c) Don't

   (d) Dont

Not all ________ agree on which parenting style to use throughout their child's life. Some believe in a more disciplined approach, while others advocate for a more lenient, understanding method. This difference in opinions often leads to debates and discussions within families. The goal for every parent, regardless of their style, is to ensure the best upbringing for their child. It is important to find a balance that works for both the parents and the child.

2. Which choice completes the text so that it conforms to the conventions of Standard English?

   (a) babies

   (b) baby's

   (c) babie's

   (d) babies'

I had to stop on the side of the road as I realized my ________ engine was making an unusual noise. The sound grew louder, indicating a potential problem that needed immediate attention. Pulling over, I opened the hood to investigate, hoping it was something minor. Unfortunately, it seemed more serious than I initially thought, requiring professional assistance. This unexpected issue disrupted my travel plans, adding a layer of stress to my day.

3. Which choice completes the text so that it conforms to the conventions of Standard English?

   (a) cars

   (b) car

   (c) car's

   (d) cars'

_______________ speech at the graduation made multiple audience members cry. His words were heartfelt, reflecting on the journey and growth experienced by the graduates. He spoke about the challenges they overcame, the friendships they formed, and the bright futures ahead. The sincerity in his voice and the personal anecdotes he shared resonated deeply with everyone present. It was a memorable moment that added a special touch to the ceremony.

4. Which choice completes the text so that it conforms to the conventions of Standard English?

(a) Peters

(b) Peter

(c) Peters's

(d) Peter's

Her _______________ house is in the Poconos near a lake. The serene location offers a perfect getaway from the hustle and bustle of city life. Surrounded by nature, the house provides a tranquil environment to relax and unwind. During the summer, they enjoy kayaking on the lake and hiking the nearby trails. The picturesque setting makes it an ideal spot for family gatherings and outdoor activities.

5. Which choice completes the text so that it conforms to the conventions of Standard English?

(a) parents

(b) parents's

(c) parent's

(d) parents'

While my test grade was given to me on Friday, the _______________ students' tests weren't graded until after the weekend. The delay caused some anxiety among my classmates, who were eager to know their results. Over the weekend, discussions about the test and possible outcomes were common topics. On Monday, the teacher finally handed back the graded tests, bringing both relief and surprise to many. It was a long wait, but eventually, everyone knew how they had performed.

6. Which choice completes the text so that it conforms to the conventions of Standard English?

(a) others'

(b) others

(c) other's

(d) otherses

The teacher appreciated all of the _______________ suggestions. Each idea contributed to improving the classroom environment and enhancing the learning experience. The students felt valued and motivated, knowing their opinions mattered. This collaborative approach fostered a sense of community and mutual respect. The resulting changes made a positive impact, benefiting everyone involved.

7. Which choice completes the text so that it conforms to the conventions of Standard English?

(a) students

(b) students'

(c) student's

(d) students's

After the movie, we went to _______________ house for dinner. His home was cozy and welcoming, with the smell of freshly cooked food filling the air. The evening was spent enjoying delicious meals and engaging in lively conversations. It was a perfect way to end the day, surrounded by good friends and great hospitality. John's culinary skills and warm atmosphere made the dinner truly memorable.

8. Which choice completes the text so that it conforms to the conventions of Standard English?

(a) John

(b) Johns

(c) John's

(d) Johns'

The committee approved the ________________ proposal unanimously. The plan was comprehensive and addressed all major concerns, gaining the support of every member. During the meeting, the manager outlined the benefits and potential impact of the proposal in detail. The thorough preparation and clear presentation made it easy for the committee to reach a consensus. The approval marked a significant step forward for the project.

9. Which choice completes the text so that it conforms to the conventions of Standard English?

   (a) managers

   (b) managers'

   (c) manager's

   (d) managers's

The new policy affects both the employees and their ________________. It aims to provide better work-life balance and additional support for family-related needs. The company recognizes the importance of a healthy home environment for its employees' overall well-being. As a result, the policy includes flexible working hours and enhanced parental leave benefits. This initiative is expected to improve employee satisfaction and productivity.

10. Which choice completes the text so that it conforms to the conventions of Standard English?

   (a) their

   (b) theirs

   (c) they're

   (d) there

Sample Problems: Solutions and Explanations

1. **Correct Answer: D** In this example, the correct format should be "actresses'" because it is plural and possessive. There are multiple actresses and it is their costumes that are being talked about. If you replace, "actresses" with their, you will realize that it is clearly plural possession. A is just plural, C and D don't exist.

2. **Correct Answer: C** In this example, the correct format should be "sailor's" because it is singular and possessive. One sailor and his hat that is being talked about. If you replace sailors with **his**, you will realize it is singular possessive. A is plural and incorrect. B is singular and is logically incorrect. D is plural possessive and there is no indication that there is more than one sailor.

Commonly Misused Words

There are certain words in the english language that sound the same but take on very different meanings and usages. While the problems aren't that common, it's important to make this distinction and be aware that these problems are very possible and come up.

Cheat: Commonly Misused Words

Accept vs except
Wave and waive
Bazaar vs bizarre
Desert vs. Dessert
Their there and they're
Precede vs. Proceed
Persecute vs. Prosecute
Its it's and its'

If you're unaware of the differences of each one, please look up the definitions and be cautious and aware of the various usages.

We won't be going through any sample problems here due to the fact that there isn't much to explain as you either know the usage or don't. Work through the problems on your own.

Practice Problems: Commonly Misused Words

My interest was ________________ when I saw the man running quickly across the street. It was a strange sight because he seemed to be in a hurry and kept looking over his shoulder. I wondered if he was being chased or if he was just late for something important. The urgency in his steps caught the attention of other pedestrians as well. Everyone stopped and stared, creating a moment of collective curiosity.

1. Which choice completes the text so that it conforms to the conventions of Standard English?

   (a) peaked

   (b) piqued

   (c) picked

   (d) pickled

The ________________ I had last night gave me a bellyache. It was delicious and rich, made with layers of cream and chocolate. However, I think I might have overindulged because I couldn't resist having a second serving. By the time I went to bed, I felt quite uncomfortable. The next morning, I decided to avoid sweets for a while to let my stomach recover.

2. Which choice completes the text so that it conforms to the conventions of Standard English?

   (a) dessert

   (b) desert

   (c) desssert

   (d) desseart

The king's ______________ was short-lived as he was murdered only 3 years after being on the throne. His reign was marked by numerous conflicts and attempts to consolidate power. Despite his efforts to establish a lasting legacy, his enemies were numerous and relentless. The palace was always filled with whispers of betrayal and plots against him. Ultimately, his inability to secure loyalty among his subjects led to his untimely demise.

3. Which choice completes the text so that it conforms to the conventions of Standard English?

   (a) rein

   (b) rain

   (c) rine

   (d) reign

______________ going to the concert together next weekend. It's going to be an amazing experience because we all love the band that's performing. We've been looking forward to this for months and have already planned our outfits. It's not just about the music, but also about spending time together and making memories. We're planning to grab dinner before the concert and maybe even hang out afterwards.

4. Which choice completes the text so that it conforms to the conventions of Standard English?

   (a) They're

   (b) Their

   (c) There

   (d) Thier

This painting will ______________ the decor in your living room perfectly. Its vibrant colors match the cushions and the overall theme of the room. The artist's use of light and shadow adds depth, making it a focal point of the space. Visitors will undoubtedly admire how well the painting ties the room together. It brings a sense of harmony and completeness to the interior design.

5. Which choice completes the text so that it conforms to the conventions of Standard English?

   (a) compliment

   (b) complement

   (c) complament

   (d) complemant

I need to ______________ my time wisely to complete all my tasks. With so many responsibilities on my plate, it's crucial to prioritize effectively. Creating a schedule helps ensure that nothing important is overlooked. By breaking down larger projects into smaller, manageable parts, I can maintain steady progress. Effective time management reduces stress and increases productivity.

6. Which choice completes the text so that it conforms to the conventions of Standard English?

   (a) allot

   (b) a lot

   (c) alot

   (d) allotment

Everyone was invited to the party ______________ James. It's unfortunate because he had been looking forward to it for weeks. He must have done something to upset the host, which led to his exclusion. The rest of us were surprised and a bit uncomfortable about the situation. It certainly cast a shadow over what was supposed to be a fun event.

7. Which choice completes the text so that it conforms to the conventions of Standard English?

   (a) accept

   (b) accept

   (c) except

   (d) expect

We can arrange the decorations in ______________ you prefer. Your input is important to make sure everything looks perfect for the event. Whether you want a more formal or casual setup, we can accommodate your preferences. It's all about creating an atmosphere that suits the occasion and makes everyone feel welcome. Let us know what you envision, and we'll bring it to life.

8. Which choice completes the text so that it conforms to the conventions of Standard English?

   (a) any way
   (b) anyway
   (c) anyways
   (d) in anyway

The screws are too ______________ to hold the shelf securely. This could pose a safety hazard if not addressed promptly. Tightening them might help temporarily, but it's likely we'll need to replace them with the correct size. Ensuring that the screws fit properly is essential for the stability of the shelf. Let's make sure we get the right hardware to avoid any accidents.

9. Which choice completes the text so that it conforms to the conventions of Standard English?

   (a) lose
   (b) lost
   (c) loosen
   (d) loose

Quotes

Quotation marks are used to indicate the exact words that someone has spoken or written. In most cases, quotation marks are placed around the entire quote, including any punctuation that belongs to it.
Example 1: "I love ice cream," said Jane.

Example 2: According to the article, "The economy is expected to grow by 3% this year."

However, what is often asked about is punctuation before and after the quotation.

Before the Quote	The end of the Quote
1. Always use a , to start the quote if the quote is not part of the sentence. 2. Don't use any punctuation if the quote is part of the sentence.	1. Periods, commas, and question marks always go inside the quotes 2. Semi-colons and colons always go outside the quotes

It's important to gain a deep understanding of each through application, so work through each sample problem thoroughly to understand the various usages.

Sample Problems

Sasha went on his first roller-coaster and sat in the front row with his friends. It had a steep drop that worried him and when the time came he shut his eyes and pleaded with his friends. His fear of heights was making him panic.________________ He finally moved his hands from his face and braced himself for the second drop.

1. Which choice completes the text so that it conforms to the conventions of Standard English?
   (a) Is it almost over he asked.
   (b) Is it almost over, he asked.
   (c) "Is it almost over," he asked.
   (d) "Is it almost over?" he asked.

Ms. Taylor is an elementary school science teacher. One of her lessons included a study on whales and their migration patterns. A student was quick to ask about other animals and Ms Taylor tried her best to answer. ________________ . She then continued with the lesson and taught about sharks and stingrays.

2. Which choice completes the text so that it conforms to the conventions of Standard English?
   (a) There are many different types of creatures in the sea
   (b) "There are many different types of creatures in the sea,"
   (c) "There are many different types of creatures in the sea",
   (d) "There are many different types of creatures in the sea"

Practice Problems: Quotes

Nick was nervous for his first day of school and his dad assured him he would make friends if he wasn't so shy. When Nick entered his classroom he promised himself he would socialize. Luckily he found himself seated next to a boy who had the same name as him, they laughed and joked about the teacher confusing them. Remembering his promise, Nick asked ______________ . Since then, Nick and Nick have become best friends and inseparable.

1. Which choice completes the text so that it conforms to the conventions of Standard English?

   (a) will you be my friend.

   (b) if will, you be my friend.

   (c) , "will you be my friend?"

   (d) "will you be my friend?"

Michael picked his brother up from school and they were on their way home when his brother begged him to buy him some fast food. Michael assured his brother their mom was making dinner at home and if he ate fast food their mom would get mad. Nonetheless, Michael's brother persisted and asked Michael to just not tell her. ______________ Michael cautioned. His brother sighed and eventually agreed, they headed straight home.

2. Which choice completes the text so that it conforms to the conventions of Standard English?

   (a) I don't think that's a good idea,

   (b) I don't think that's a good idea

   (c) "I don't think that's a good idea",

   (d) "I don't think that's a good idea,"

Saskia and Charlotte were on their way to a birthday party when they realized they were running late and wouldn't have time to take the train. Thus, Charlotte went and ordered a taxi to drive them to the venue. While in the car, they got stuck in traffic and the driver and Charlotte conversed about the long wait times to exit the highway. Saskia interrupted and asked ______________ . The driver assured them they would only be five minutes late. In the end, Charlotte and Saskia missed an hour of the party.

3. Which choice completes the text so that it conforms to the conventions of Standard English?

   (a) , if they will still get there on time"?

   (b) if they will still get there on time.

   (c) , if they will still get there on time?

   (d) , "if they will still get there on time?"

Mark Twain once famously quipped ______________ his words continue to inspire those who believe in the power of self-directed learning. Twain's quote emphasizes the difference between formal education and true learning. It suggests that real education extends beyond the confines of a classroom and is a lifelong process. His perspective encourages individuals to seek knowledge through their own experiences and curiosity. This quote remains relevant today, reminding us that education is not limited to what is taught in schools, but also what we learn on our own.

4. Which choice completes the text so that it conforms to the conventions of Standard English?

   (a) , "I have never let my schooling interfere with my education";

   (b) "I have never let my schooling interfere with my education";

   (c) , "I have never let my schooling interfere with my education;"

   (d) I have never let my schooling interfere with my education

Bobby and Sam were on a field trip at the zoo going through the exhibits together. While on the bus ride home they talked about their favorite animals. Sam expressed that he loved the otters because of how energetic they were. Sam then asked Bobby what exhibit he enjoyed visiting the most. Bobby replied ________________ . They couldn't wait to go home and tell their families about their trip.

5. Which choice completes the text so that it conforms to the conventions of Standard English?

   (a) the monkeys were my favorite.

   (b) ": the monkeys were my favorite."

   (c) , "the monkeys were my favorite."

   (d) , "the monkeys were my favorite".

Melissa decided to check her daughter's grades after finding out she didn't do well on her math exam. Melissa had been reassured by her daughter that she was doing well at school but her daughter's report card caught her by surprise. ________________ Melissa immediately called a tutoring place and scheduled weekly lessons to improve her daughter's scores.

6. Which choice completes the text so that it conforms to the conventions of Standard English?

   (a) "I've had it up to here!" she screamed.

   (b) I've had it up to here, "she screamed!"

   (c) I've had it up to here, she screamed!

   (d) I've had it up to here: she screamed!

Albert Einstein once said ________________ his insights continue to influence modern physics. His quote underscores the value of creativity in scientific endeavors. Einstein believed that imagination allows us to envision possibilities beyond the current boundaries of knowledge. This philosophy has inspired countless scientists to pursue innovative approaches in their research. His words remind us that while knowledge is essential, it is the power of imagination that drives progress and discovery.

7. Which choice completes the text so that it conforms to the conventions of Standard English?

   (a) , "Imagination is more important than knowledge";

   (b) "Imagination is more important than knowledge";

   (c) , "Imagination is more important than knowledge."

   (d) Imagination is more important than knowledge

During the meeting, Sarah exclaimed ________________ everyone agreed with her statement. Her enthusiasm was contagious, and her colleagues couldn't help but share in her excitement. The project's success was a result of months of hard work and collaboration. Sarah's declaration was a moment of collective triumph, highlighting the team's dedication and perseverance. The room buzzed with a sense of achievement and optimism for future endeavors.

8. Which choice completes the text so that it conforms to the conventions of Standard English?

   (a) , "This project is a huge success!";

   (b) "This project is a huge success!";

   (c) , "This project is a huge success!"

   (d) This project is a huge success

The instructor reminded the class ______________ the students made a note of the deadline. This was a crucial reminder because the assignment was a significant part of their final grade. The instructor emphasized the importance of starting early to avoid last-minute stress. Many students nodded in agreement, acknowledging the need for proper time management. By the end of the class, everyone was aware of the upcoming deadline and the expectations associated with it.

9. Which choice completes the text so that it conforms to the conventions of Standard English?

   (a) , "The assignment is due next Friday";

   (b) , "The assignment is due next Friday."

   (c) The assignment is due next Friday

   (d) "The assignment is due next Friday";

Tom told his friends ______________ they all started laughing. His story was so unexpected and outlandish that they couldn't help but be amused. Tom swore he saw strange lights and shapes in the sky, making dramatic gestures as he described the encounter. His friends teased him, suggesting he might have been dreaming or mistaken. Despite their skepticism, Tom insisted it was a real experience, adding to the humor of the situation.

10. Which choice completes the text so that it conforms to the conventions of Standard English?

   (a) , "I saw a UFO last night";

   (b) , "I saw a UFO last night."

   (c) "I saw a UFO last night";

   (d) I saw a UFO last night

Sample Problems: Solutions and Explanations

1. **Correct Answer: D** In this example, the question mark must be inside the quotes and there is no comma before "he" because you can't have two forms of punctuation next to one another. Choice A and B are incorrect because you must include the quotation marks around "Is it almost over" because it is a direct statement of what "he asked." and does not belong to the sentence. Choice C is incorrect because it is a question.

2. **Correct Answer: B** In this example, the comma must go before the quotation mark because this is a direct quotation and does not belong to the sentence. Choice C is incorrect because you **always** include the comma inside the quote. D is incorrect because you need the comma to separate the clauses.

Answer Key

Chapter 1 Answers

Transition Words Chapter: Answers

1. D	3. B	5. A	7. C	9. B
2. D	4. A	6. A	8. C	10. A

Dangling Modifiers Chapter: Answers

1. C	3. B	5. B	7. C	9. C
2. D	4. A	6. C	8. A	10. A

Commonly Used Words After Commas Chapter: Answers

1. D	3. C	5. A	7. D	9. D
2. C	4. D	6. B	8. C	10. A

Appositives Chapter: Answers

1. C	3. C	5. B	7. A	9. D
2. D	4. A	6. B	8. C	10. D

Comma Nouns/Pronouns Chapter: Answers

1. A	3. C	5. A	7. B	9. C
2. D	4. A	6. A	8. A	10. A

SemiColons Chapter: Answers

1. B	3. D	5. C	7. B	9. A
2. A	4. B	6. A	8. C	10. A

Conjunctions Chapter: Answers

1. C	3. C	5. B	7. D	9. B
2. D	4. A	6. C	8. A	10. C

Colons Chapter: Answers

1. C	3. A	5. B	7. A	9. A
2. B	4. B	6. B	8. C	10. C

Hyphens Chapter: Answers

1. C
2. A
3. C
4. B
5. A
6. C
7. B
8. D
9. A
10. D

Parentheses Chapter: Answers

1. C
2. A
3. D
4. A
5. C
6. C
7. D
8. D
9. B
10. B

Who/Whom Chapter: Answers

1. A
2. C
3. A
4. B
5. C
6. C
7. B
8. A
9. B
10. A

Affect vs. Effect Chapter: Answers

1. A
2. C
3. D
4. A
5. C
6. B
7. A
8. A
9. B
10. B

Concision Chapter: Answers

1. D
2. C
3. B
4. D
5. A
6. D
7. B
8. A
9. C
10. D

Replace a Pronoun with a Noun Chapter: Answers

1. B
2. B
3. A
4. B
5. A
6. D
7. A
8. A
9. B
10. D

I vs. Me Chapter: Answers

1. C
2. B
3. D
4. B
5. B
6. B
7. A
8. C
9. A
10. A

Verb Tense Consistency Chapter: Answers

1. B
2. A
3. C
4. A
5. D
6. C
7. B
8. A
9. D
10. B

False Comparison Chapter: Answers

1. B
2. D
3. A
4. D
5. D
6. A
7. B
8. A
9. A
10. B

Apostrophe Chapter: Answers

1. B
2. D
3. C
4. D
5. D
6. A
7. B
8. C
9. C
10. A

Commonly Misused Words Chapter: Answers

1. B
2. A
3. D
4. C
5. A
6. B
7. C
8. A
9. D
10.

Quotes Chapter: Answers

1. C
2. D
3. A
4. B
5. C
6. A
7. C
8. B
9. D
10. C

Printed in Great Britain
by Amazon

44980452R00057